TWAYNE'S WORLD AUTHORS SERIES

A Survey of the World's Literature

Sylvia E. Bowman, Indiana University

GENERAL EDITOR

AUSTRIA

Ulrich Weisstein, Indiana University

EDITOR

Karl Kraus

(TWAS 116)

TWAYNE'S WORLD AUTHORS SERIES (TWAS)

*The purpose of TWAS is to survey the major
writers—novelists, dramatists, historians, poets,
philosophers, and critics—of the nations of the world.
Among the national literatures covered are those of
Australia, Canada, China, Eastern Europe, France,
Germany, Greece, India, Italy, Japan, Latin America,
New Zealand, Poland, Russia, Scandinavia, Spain, and
the African nations, as well as Hebrew, Yiddish, and
Latin Classical literatures. This survey is comple-
mented by Twayne's United States Authors Series
and English Authors Series.*

*The intent of each volume in these series is to present
a critical-analytical study of the works of the writer;
to include biographical and historical material that
may be necessary for understanding, appreciation,
and critical appraisal of the writer; and to present all
material in clear, concise English—but not to vitiate
the scholarly content of the work by doing so.*

KARL KRAUS

By HARRY ZOHN
Brandeis University

Twayne Publishers, Inc. : : New York

To Judy

The passage on pages 32-33 from Robert Musil's *The Man Without Qualities,* vol. 1, translated by Eithne Wilkins and Ernst Kaiser, is reprinted by permission of Coward-McCann, Inc. (© 1953).

Preface

To write about Karl Kraus in a language other than his own is a difficult and dubious undertaking. As Erich Heller has put it, "Karl Kraus did not write 'in a language,' but through him the beauty, profundity, and accumulated moral experience of the German language assumed personal shape and became the crucial witness in the case this inspired prosecutor brought against his time." [1] The presentation of this "case"—as well as the case of Karl Kraus—is bound to suffer in translation and transplantation. The essential untranslatability of this writer has long been axiomatic. Only a small fraction of his extensive literary output has appeared in English: a selection from his poetry, now utterly unobtainable (*Poems,* translated by Albert Bloch; Boston: Four Seas Co., 1930); a scene from Kraus's dramatic magnum opus, *Die letzten Tage der Menschheit* (in Max Spalter, *Brecht's Tradition;* Baltimore: Johns Hopkins Press, 1967); and a few dozen aphorisms (in *The Viking Book of Aphorisms,* W. H. Auden and Louis Kronenberger, eds.; New York: Viking Press, 1962 and *The New Book of Unusual Quotations,* Rudolf Flesch, ed.; New York: Harper & Row, 1966). In the absence of serviceable English versions of an author's major works, any statement as to his stature and relevance cannot be adequately documented for English-speaking readers and must largely be taken on faith.

The vitriolic Viennese satirist, who hauled the powerful and the pitiful alike before a tribunal of total satire, was a legend in his lifetime. Following a decade of desuetude, his works have been rediscovered and republished after the Second World War. Once again Kraus is widely discussed, although it must be observed that the literature on him still ranges from panegyrics to vilification and that objective assessments are the exception rather than the rule. Among the numerous studies that have appeared in recent years are two books in English—Wilma Iggers' *Karl Kraus: A Viennese Critic of the Twentieth Century* and Frank Field's *The Last Days of Mankind: Karl Kraus and His Vienna.* The present study is intended as an introduction to Kraus; concentrating on his life, on his personality, and on the various aspects of his creativeness, it aims at presenting a more detailed discussion of his major writings than has appeared in most other studies, particularly those in English. The periodical *Die Fackel,* which contains most of Kraus's work, has long been a rarity, and even the new edition which the Kösel-Verlag began to issue in 1968 will find its way into relatively few libraries. Therefore quotations are, wherever possible, drawn from the fourteen readily available postwar collections of Kraus's writings. Unless otherwise credited, the translations from Kraus and others, including the Aphoristic Sampler, are by the author of this book.

Egon Friedell called Kraus's writings "a fanatically imaginative, superhumanly delineated work which will permanently preserve the traits of our age."[2] With superior artistry, Kraus fashioned the imperishable profile of his time from highly perishable materials, basing the permanent record of an age on transitory papers. "I have to wait until my writings are obsolete," he once wrote; "then they may acquire timeliness."[3] Paradoxically enough, this dictum (or contradiction) by Kraus seems to be coming true. May this book make a modest contribution toward clarifying this process.

HARRY ZOHN

Brandeis University

Contents

Acknowledgments

Anyone who is interested in Karl Kraus owes a debt of gratitude to Heinrich Fischer and to the Kösel-Verlag of Munich, the editor and the publisher of the fine postwar editions of most of Kraus's writings. My specific gratitude is for their permission to present excerpts from Kraus's works in English translation. Professor Ulrich Weisstein has put me in his debt with his promptly and graciously given editorial care. Mrs. Albert Bloch kindly permitted me to examine and use her late husband's revisions of his translations from Kraus. The secretarial assistance provided by Brandeis University is also gratefully acknowledged.

CHRONOLOGY

1874	Karl Kraus is born at Jičin (Bohemia) on April 28.
1877	His family moves to Vienna
1884– 1892	Kraus attends the Franz-Josephs-Gymnasium.
1891	First theatrical activities. Death of his mother (October 24).
1892– 1898	Kraus attends the University of Vienna.
1896	*Die demolirte Literatur.*
1898	*Eine Krone für Zion.*
1899	Kraus publishes the first issue of *Die Fackel* on April 1. Leaves the Jewish fold (October 12).
1900	Death of his father on April 5.
1901	Death of Annie Kalmar on May 2.
1902	"Sittlichkeit und Kriminalität" (essay).
1908	*Sittlichkeit und Kriminalität* (collection).
1909	*Sprüche und Widersprüche.*
1910	First public reading from his own writings. *Heine und die Folgen. Die chinesische Mauer.*
1911	Kraus is baptized on April 8.
1912	*Nestroy und die Nachwelt. Pro domo et mundo.*
1913	Kraus meets Sidonie Nadherny.
1914	"In dieser grossen Zeit . . ."
1915	Kraus begins work on *Die letzten Tage der Menschheit.* Kurt Wolff founds the Verlag der Schriften von Karl Kraus.
1916	First volume of *Worte in Versen.*
1918	*Nachts.*
1918– 1919	*Die letzten Tage der Menschheit* appears in special issues of the *Fackel.*
1919	*Weltgericht.*
1921	*Literatur oder Man wird doch da sehn.*
1922	First Nestroy cycle. *Traumstück. Untergang der Welt durch schwarze Magie.*
1923	Kraus officially leaves the Catholic church (March 7). *Wolkenkuckucksheim.*

1924	*Traumtheater.*
1925	Beginning of Békessy polemics. Kraus designates his recitals "Theater der Dichtung."
1926	First presentation of Offenbach operettas.
1927	Massacre in Vienna (July). Polemic against police chief Schober. *Epigramme.*
1928	*Die Unüberwindlichen.*
1929	*Literatur und Lüge.*
1930– 1932	Broadcasts of Offenbach and Shakespeare adaptations.
1931	*Zeitstrophen.*
1933	Work on *Die Dritte Walpurgisnacht.*
1933– 1935	Shakespeare's *Sonette* and *Dramen.*
1936	The last *Fackel* appears (February). Kraus dies in Vienna on June 12.

CHAPTER 1

A Life Between Love and Hate

KARL KRAUS was born on April 28, 1874, in Jičin (Jitschin or Gitschin in German), a small Bohemian town northeast of Prague. The place is of some historical significance as the favorite residence of Albrecht Wenzel von Wallenstein, the celebrated general of the Thirty Years' War. In 1866 Bismarck had stayed in the house in which the boy was born. At the age of fifty Kraus had occasion to reply to a man who had made derogatory remarks about his native town: "It is a clean place with scenic and cultural attractions, venerable as the scene of bloody events and because of its wealth of historical buildings; in the vicinity is the 'Charterhouse of Gitschin' which is mentioned by Schiller, formerly the burial place of Wallenstein. . . ."[1]

Karl Kraus was the ninth and second-youngest child, the fifth son, of Jakob and Ernestine (Kantor) Kraus. His father, of a petty bourgeois background, was a well-to-do businessman, a manufacturer of paper bags; later he became the owner of a paper factory and acquired additional business interests. The family business was so solid that it was able to survive the economic crash of 1873 and outlasted its owner by several decades. Here was a family constellation that was typical at the turn of the century: the sons of Central European Jewish businessmen—often self-made men, strong and self-willed, heads of patriarchally organized families—turned to literature. Cases in point are Franz Kafka, Stefan Zweig, Siegfried Trebitsch, Felix Salten, and Franz Werfel. Karl Kraus differed from most of these in that his father, although not oriented toward literature, did not disapprove of his son's early thespian and literary pursuits and did not attempt to put any impediments in his path. As a child, Karl Kraus was delicate, shy, and sickly, giving early indications of curvature of the spine and of myopia. His father seems to have been a responsible person whose sternness was tempered by a marked sense of humor. The mother, a daughter of the physician Ignaz Kantor, died as early as 1891; Karl remembered her fondly for the rest of his life.[2]

In 1877 the family moved to Vienna, and despite his deeply ingrained aversion to the noise and traffic of a big city and his fear of crossing busy streets, Karl Kraus was to spend the rest of his life there. Berlin was the only other city he ever considered as a residence. His childhood was a generally happy one, and later he returned to it in a number of his finest poems.[3] On his visits to the *Stadtpark,* perhaps the loveliest of Vienna's municipal parks, the boy would take along, for comfort and security, his most precious possession, a puppet theater. He enjoyed grade school, the outings in the Vienna Woods, and the summers at Weidlingau. From 1884 on, he attended the Franz-Josephs-Gymnasium, where his schoolmates included the writers Karl Rosner and Hugo Bettauer. Of his siblings he got along best with his oldest brother, Richard, who died in 1909 (Richard's daughter was Kraus's favorite niece), and his younger sister Marie.[4]

Kraus's favorite teacher was Heinrich Sedlmayer, a man whom years later he remembered fondly and gratefully in a poem entitled "To An Old Teacher" (Henricus Stephanus Sedlmayer).[5] This teacher's subjects were German and Latin, and Kraus later credited his study of Latin with laying the groundwork for his appreciation of style. His teacher of religion, however, was a bad one—a pedantic, insensitive, orthodox man who rewarded the religious doubts and gropings of his charges with low grades.

Kraus's good memory, which was reputed to have extended to the third year of his life, made him a good reciter at school. His parodistic and mimic talents asserted themselves at an early age; they were fed by the impulses he received at the old Burgtheater, the Imperial Theater which was torn down in 1888 and rebuilt at its present location. Kraus often expressed his admiration of actors and actresses like Adolf von Sonnenthal, Charlotte Wolter, Ludwig and Zerline Gabillon, Bernhard Baumeister, Ernst and Helene Hartmann, and Friedrich Mitterwurzer. In the actor Alexander Girardi he saw the quintessence of a bygone Vienna, with its lightheartedness, warmth, simplicity, and wit. By 1891 the young man wrote, directed, and acted in dramatic sketches. In those years, Kraus's life, like that of so many fledgling *littérateurs,* centered about the theater and coffeehouses like the Café Griensteidl, which he frequented with Rosner and other friends. Like many of his contemporaries, he applauded writers like Detlev von Liliencron and Gerhart Hauptmann, who were fighting against social mendacity and the falsification of nature.

In 1892 Kraus completed his secondary education with the *Matura* examination; his grades were only mediocre. At his father's request, he enrolled at the University of Vienna in December of that year as a law student, but he attended few lectures. In 1894 he switched to courses in philosophy and German literature, attending the university until 1898 without, however, taking a degree. Since the emptiness of the coffeehouse atmosphere soon revolted him, Kraus strove to find and express truth as an actor. In January, 1893, he played the role of the villainous Franz Moor in Schiller's play *Kabale und Liebe.* His failure as an actor definitely and irrevocably turned him to journalism and literature, although his mimic talents later asserted themselves in the numerous dramatic readings which he gave in his one-man "Theater of Poetry."

While still a schoolboy, Kraus had contributed a "Letter from Ischl" to *Das Rendezvous,* a new illustrated review. In 1892 he began to contribute book reviews and theatrical critiques to *Die Gesellschaft,* the respected Leipzig journal and organ of the literary Naturalists. Having offered his services to Jakob Lippowitz, the founder of the *Neues Wiener Journal,* without success, he now wrote for the *Breslauer Zeitung,* the *Wiener Literatur-Zeitung,* the *Wiener Rundschau,* the *Neue literarische Blätter* of Bremen, *Die Zeit* (Vienna), and other newspapers and journals. To *Die Gesellschaft* and the Viennese journal *Liebelei* he contributed reviews and satirical sketches under the pseudonym "Crêpe de Chine," but his writings were soon made of sterner stuff.

His early success and a degree of prominence are indicated by Kraus's inclusion in *Das geistige Wien (Intellectual Vienna),* a list of writers and artists whose author described Kraus in 1893 as being "active in the areas of drama, criticism, and satire."[6] Such early notice may be regarded as uncommon in an age which did not ordinarily accord recognition to young intellectuals. Eisenberg's dictionary stated that Kraus was editor of a *Satirenanthologie.* Kraus had actually planned such an annual anthology together with Anton Lindner, but not a single volume appeared—presumably owing to a dearth of suitable material. Kraus later wrote that his Storm and Stress period took the form of establishing and cultivating literary and journalistic "connections" with a view toward earning a living within the framework of liberal journalism. In those years he dreamed of becoming the successor of Daniel Spitzer, whose witty column "Wiener Spaziergänge" ("Viennese Perambulations") had regularly appeared in the prestigious daily *Neue Freie Presse* until Spitzer's death in 1893. Between 1894 and 1896 Kraus did indeed contribute to that newspaper.

Kraus's first major satire, *Die demolirte Literatur (The Demolished Literature)*, first appeared in the *Wiener Rundschau* at the end of 1896 and was such a success that it netted Kraus a physical attack from one of the writers he had lampooned—his erstwhile coffeehouse companion Felix Salten. In 1898 Kraus became an editor of the weekly *Die Wage*, and this position enabled him to get to know journalism from within. He was to attack the press and its practitioners for the rest of his life. Kraus had the feeling that he was living in a particularly difficult age for the satirist: his contemporaries were so ludicrous that they did not realize how laughable they were and had no ear for laughter. It was Kraus's basic intention to put his age between quotation marks. Quotation is the hallmark of his satire, and in its use he was guided by the insight that what was most unspeakable about his age could be spoken only by the age itself.

Since work within the "Establishment" seemed to Kraus to be hedged in with multifarious taboos and considerations of a personal and commercial nature, he decided to found his own journal. When Moriz Benedikt, the co-owner and editor-in-chief of the *Neue Freie Presse*, learned of this in January of 1899, he offered his sometime contributor the post vacated by Daniel Spitzer—presumably that of chief satirical writer. (According to some sources, the post was that of *Feuilletonredakteur* or cultural editor, a position held, until his death in 1904, by Theodor Herzl, the father of political Zionism. Even though Herzl was by then immersed in far-ranging outside activities and had reason to fear that the neglect of his duties would cost him his job, Kraus does not seem to have been considered for his job and is, in any case, not mentioned in Herzl's voluminous and extremely candid published *Diaries*).

By that time Kraus had already attacked Herzl, the Zionist *and* the journalist, in his second pamphlet, *Eine Krone für Zion (A Crown for Zion*, 1898). Making a very crucial decision, Kraus turned this flattering job offer down. "There are two fine things in the world: to be part of the *Neue Freie Presse* or to despise it. I did not hesitate for one moment as to what my choice had to be."[7] Apart from the fact that even then he had learned to loathe the combination of business and art which, to his mind, the *Neue Freie Presse* represented in particularly striking form, Kraus must have felt that he had to be an outsider, a loner, to mount meaningful attacks on what he regarded as the pernicious press.

The first issue of Kraus's magazine *Die Fackel (The Torch)* appeared on April 1, 1899. This publication turned out to be as long-lived as it was aggressive. Setting out to "drain a swamp of clichés,"[8] Kraus at first enlisted the services of numerous writers, but from the very first issue he wrote about two-thirds of the contents himself. From 1911 to 1936 the *Fackel* was exclusively his own work.

The Dreyfus affair having signaled for many the failure of assimilation, Kraus left the Jewish fold in October, 1899, and for some years remained *konfessionslos,* that is, religiously unaffiliated. He made no public announcement of this move or of his conversion to Catholicism in April, 1911 ("I don't like to meddle in my private affairs"[9]), and his readers were not informed until 1922, when he left the church again. Despite being ignored by the liberal press, which was predominantly owned and staffed by Jews, and attacked by the less gifted and less influential anti-Semitic (Christian-Socialist or German-Nationalist) papers, Kraus soon became influential and feared. After the death of his father in the spring of 1900, Kraus detached himself from his family and moved into an apartment of his own. Since he received a subvention from his family, his financial independence enabled him to make no concessions to popular taste—except at the very beginning, when he did accept paid advertisements in the *Fackel.*

If Kraus's early satiric writings were directed largely against standard aspects of corruption, the second period of his creativity may be dated from the appearance of his essay "Sittlichkeit und Kriminalität" ("Morality and Criminality") in 1902. (This work became the title essay of a book-length collection which appeared in 1908.) With this essay Kraus evinced an interest in a new theme, the problem of the separation between the public and the private spheres of an individual's life. In particular, Kraus saw the individual endangered by the state's interference with a free and private sexual life. Undoubtedly his thinking and feeling about this subject had been shaped by his relationship to the young actress Annie Kalmar, whom he had met in the summer of 1900 and who died of tuberculosis in Hamburg in May, 1901, aged twenty-three. Kraus's affection for this talented young woman, the first of several women of striking physical and spiritual beauty in his life, was misinterpreted in various circles, and the journalist Bernhard Buchbinder, who had vilified Annie Kalmar's memory, was successfully sued by the mother of the deceased actress.

The book edition of *Sittlichkeit und Kriminalität* was followed by the pamphlets *Heine und die Folgen* (*Heine and the Consequences,* 1910) and *Nestroy und die Nachwelt* (*Nestroy and Posterity,* 1912) and the books *Die chinesische Mauer* (*The Great Wall of China*, 1910), *Sprüche und Widersprüche* (*Dicta and Contradictions*, 1909) and *Pro domo et mundo* (1912). The success of these works, coupled with the fact that, from 1910 on, the satirist gave public readings from his own works and those of other writers, made Kraus a public figure despite the wall of silence by which the Austrian press strove to isolate him. Kraus smarted under the yoke of this status, resenting popular appellations like *"Fackelkraus"* and what he regarded as invasions of his privacy. He suffered when people accosted him in a café, on the street, or on a train,[10] and he preferred traveling by car or by plane even at a time when these modes of transportation were rather uncommon.

In the spirit of George Bernard Shaw's dictum that the world's best reformers are those who begin on themselves, Kraus tried to lead an exemplary life, a kind of "public life" that was intended to be blameless, wholly consistent, and almost ascetic, a life that would serve the work he was trying to do and be entirely in keeping with it. To an extent that is rare in literature, Karl Kraus's life was his work and his writings constitute his biography. With rare courage and consistency, and in marked contrast to the "timelessness" of ivory-tower poets, Kraus made himself the measure of the unworthiness of his age, of his era's moral bankruptcy. He strove to be a shining light of integrity in a morass of dubious morality, a beacon of genuineness in a sea of spuriousness.

Far from being accidental or merely eccentric, Kraus's working habits were one more aspect of his opposition to his time, of the satirist's self-imposed burden.[11] In the evening, he would go to a café[12] and read the newspapers, the primary source material of the man bent upon pinning down his age between quotation marks and literally taking it at its word. (Walter Benjamin had Kraus's ingestion of newspapers in mind when he referred to his "fire-eating, sword-swallowing philology of the journals.")[13] After conversing with a few friends, Kraus would work all night, sifting the world through the sieve of the word—to use his own phrase.[14] Using a cheap wooden pen holder and a steel nib, Kraus covered one blank proofsheet after another with his minuscule handwriting, which only a very few typesetters were able to decipher.[15]

Kraus's printer used to call in the morning for what had been written during the night, and on the next evening the galleys were already on his desk for his revision and emendation. Some of his writings had to be set in type ten or twelve times before he gave his final approval ("No one who sees one of my works in print will recognize a seam. And yet everything was torn open a hundred times.")[16] As it was for Franz Kafka, writing was a necessary therapy for Karl Kraus. In one of his most characteristic and poignant poems, he alludes not only to his working habits, to what has been called the "claustrophobic intensity of his work,"[17] but to the recalcitrant material with which he had to work and live.

Nocturnal Hour

Nocturnal hour that passes from me,
the while I devise it and turn it and tend it,
and this long night shall soon be ended.
Outside a bird says: it is day.

Nocturnal hour that passes from me,
the while I devise it and turn it and tend it,
and this long winter shall soon be ended.
Outside a bird says: it is spring.

Nocturnal hour that passes from me,
the while I devise it and turn it and tend it,
and this long life shall soon be ended.
Outside a bird says: it is death.[18]

In his private life, Kraus was, by most accounts, kindly, uncomplicated, natural, and charming rather than egocentric, petty, or irascible. While he did not lack friends, his existence was basically and of necessity a lonely one. He never married. In 1913 he met Baroness Sidonie Nadherny von Borutin, a sensitive, artistic, nature-loving young woman of great beauty. Kraus was a frequent guest at her family estate, Janovice Castle at Vrchotovy Janovice (Janowitz), south of Prague. Despite his recorded opposition to family ties and marriage ("Since the law prohibits the keeping of wild animals and I get no enjoyment from pets, I prefer to remain unmarried"),[19] it is known that Kraus proposed marriage to "Sidie" Nadherny several times between 1913 and 1915. Class differences and possibly Kraus's Jewish origin appear to have stood in the way of such a union.[20]

In 1920 Sidonie Nadherny married a physician, Count Max von Thun und Hohenstein; but the marriage was soon dissolved, and Sidonie returned to live at her castle with her twin brother Karl. Except for one period of estrangement (1918 to 1921), Kraus's affectionate relationship with her continued until his death. Again and again, the satirist found relaxation and inspiration on the beautiful Nadherny estate or on trips taken with Sidonie. She represented beauty to him and gave him the strength to endure what he regarded as the shame of his time. There are multifarious dedications and allusions to her in his poetic work.[21] Between 1913 and 1936 Kraus addressed about a thousand letters, cards, and telegrams to her. Long presumed lost, this collection was rediscovered in 1969 and is scheduled for publication in 1971.[22]

The outbreak of the war in 1914 marked a turning point in Kraus's life and creativity, and the outraged convictions of the pacifist inspired the satirist to produce his most powerful and characteristic work. After June, 1914, when everyone else seemed to be talking and writing at a furious pace, Kraus fell silent for several months. He finally broke the silence with his public lecture of November 19, "In dieser grossen Zeit. . . ." ("In these great times. . . ."), other lectures in December, 1914 and February, 1915, and a 168-page issue of *Die Fackel* in October, 1915. "In this chaos," writes Leopold Liegler, "Karl Kraus was one of the few who courageously and clearly expressed the meaning of all these horrors, this bestiality that had become duty. He disenchanted those who had allowed themselves to be bedazzled by the enthusiasm of the first months of the war; he consoled and comforted those who despaired and let them know at least that there existed bonds of spirit and faith that united these individuals."[23] Having been rejected for army duty for physical reasons, Kraus largely escaped censorship by his method of juxtaposing various statements and turning the spotlight of language on them. For Kraus war was hell on earth, a desecration of creation itself and the farthest imaginable point from the *Ursprung,* the origin. Paul Schick writes, "Since he believed in an absolute decision between good and evil, he was convinced that liberation from evil could come only through recognition and profound atonement, from a definitive rejection of all half-truths, all compromises with evil. His work in wartime can be understood only with reference to this belief, born of hope and despair. It is not only satire that unmasked, but, above all, a confession of faith."[24]

Apart from the contents of one hundred issues of *Die Fackel* issued during the war years, Kraus's greatest wartime creation, and certainly the most striking work in his whole oeuvre, is the pacifist play *Die letzten Tage der Menschheit (The Last Days of Mankind),* a corrosive catalogue of the sins of mankind, with a marked Austrian—and, to a lesser extent, German—flavor. Kraus was well aware that an individual was powerless to stop a world conflagration with his pen. "Nevertheless," he wrote in his preface to the play, "such a complete confession of the guilt of belonging to this mankind must be welcome somewhere and of use some day." [25]

In addition to his anguish for misled mankind, Kraus suffered a number of grievous personal losses in wartime. In 1917 the dancer Elisabeth Reitler—like her sister Helene Kann a friend of Kraus's—, committed suicide because she could no longer bear the horrors of the war (*Nachts*, a collection of aphorisms, is dedicated to her memory); in July, 1917, Kraus's friend, the art historian Franz Grüner, was killed in the war; in November of that year, the same fate befell the talented Czech-born poet Franz Janowitz, whose work and friendship Kraus treasured; and soon thereafter his favorite nephew, Stefan Fridezko, became a casualty. [26]

When there was danger that Italy would enter the war, Kraus went to Rome in March, 1915, to utilize some personal contacts in an effort to prevent the spread of the carnage. Having been unsuccessful, he spent the summer months at Janovice. Later he made several trips to Switzerland with Sidonie; in Thierfehd he wrote the Epilogue to *Die letzten Tage der Menschheit*. Indeed, many of his poems, written in an idyllic atmosphere, reflect the contrast between the divine calm of nature and the man-made carnage of wartime.

After the war, the essentially apolitical satirist Kraus thought he saw some hope in the policies and practices of the Social Democratic party, calling "the headlong plunge of conservative thought into a chaos in which it could act only as the dreadful beadle of a world view bitterly opposed to it" his "unparalleled experience in this time." [27] On May 1, 1919, Karl Seitz, the head of the National Assembly, wrote on the occasion of the twentieth anniversary of *Die Fackel:* "Every friend of the Republic will gratefully acknowledge what your writings have contributed to the exorcism of the old ghosts." [28] Kraus was not sure that the old ghosts had indeed been exorcised, for the journalists of the old stripe were still around, and in them he saw a root evil. In 1922 Kraus left the Catholic Church. For one thing, the Church had disappointed him in wartime, and then he had hoped that under Pope Benedict XV, in whom he saw the embodiment of a true Christian philosophy, it would live up to its religious and humanitarian mission. Instead, he saw it joining what he regarded as the unholy trinity: Political Power—Journalism—Business. The news that the Salzburg Cathedral had been made available to Max Reinhardt for mounting Hugo von Hofmannsthal's modern morality play *Jedermann* on its square as an annual tourist attraction provided the occasion for breaking with the Church.[29] (The act was officially recorded on March 7, 1923.)

In August, 1924, on the tenth anniversary of the outbreak of the world war, Kraus wrote a piece analogous to his celebrated speech of 1914, "In dieser kleinen Zeit" ("In These Small Times"), predicting that the times would become "great" again.

If this were not so, the attempt of the devil to brand them with the swastika would have failed on the first day. . . . Always those romanticists will be on top who reach for the sword, which is a hand grenade, and call to the colors, which are flames, so that they can accuse the victims of a gas attack of having violated dress regulations.[30]

Kraus's Cassandra cries, however, fell on deaf ears in a period of beginning political and economic stabilization. A few years later came Kraus's almost single-handed crusade against the machinations of Imre Békessy, a corrupt journalist and manipulator who had founded several publications intended to give him control of Austria's political, economic, and cultural life. This fight, coupled with Kraus's attacks on Johann Schober—then Vienna's chief of police—in connection with a massacre on the streets of Vienna in 1927, found its literary expression in the play *Die Unüberwindlichen* (*The Unconquerable Ones,* 1928). Once again Kraus wished to appeal to the conscience of a moral island, continuing to believe that his attitude was to be an example for many and that the battle, no matter how great the odds, was not lost as long as he was there to fight it. His main problem was that reality kept outdistancing satire, and in those years Kraus had a constant sense of the impending apocalypse as well as a feeling of growing isolation. His "Grabschrift" ("Epitaph"), written in 1930, reflects this mood.

> How empty it is here
> In my place.
> All striving wasted
> Nothing of me remains
> But the source
> Which was not given.[31]

(The "source" presumably refers to the spirit from which this wasted striving sprang; the line carries an additional allusion to the use and misuse of Kraus's work by others.)

In specific terms, the Social Democrats' kowtowing to their real enemies (such as Schober, who had become Austria's prime minister) led Kraus to write that "since mankind has let itself be cheated by politics, there has never been a greater failure than the activities of this party." [32] In 1932 Kraus attended an international pacifist congress in Amsterdam together with Romain Rolland, Henri Barbusse, Frans Masereel, Albert Einstein, Heinrich Mann, John Dos Passos, Upton Sinclair, and Maxim Gorky, serving as the only Austrian on the committee.

The rise of National Socialism brought Kraus further conflicts and anguish. In the face of the Nazi menace across the German border, he hailed Engelbert Dollfuss, the diminutive Austrian chancellor, as "the small savior from the great danger, the David who would beat Goliath." [33] This turned out to be both a naïve and a vain hope, but the relatively unpolitical Kraus continued to cling to his belief in the dominance and power of a great personality. In those years Kraus found himself increasingly isolated and vilified, since both his admirers and detractors believed that the extraordinary times called for unequivocal expressions from intellectuals; instead, Kraus made satirical sallies against his usual targets and, in the view of many observers, kept blurring the real issues.

One of his targets was the press, and in the memorable *Fackel* No. 890–905 he wrote: "National Socialism did not destroy the press; rather, the press created National Socialism—seemingly as a reaction, but actually as a fulfillment." [34] A few days after this issue of *Die Fackel* had appeared, Dollfuss was assassinated, and Kraus was profoundly shaken. In February, 1933 heart trouble had been diagnosed; and a year later phlebitis appeared. In his despair Kraus turned to *Sprachlehre* (the study of language) and made efforts to establish a language seminar "which, by presenting horrors of syntax, would aim at getting closer to the possibilities, and thus the mysteries, of the most profound language, whose obscene use has led to the horrors of blood." [35]

The last issue of the *Fackel* appeared in February, 1936. That month Kraus was struck down in the darkness by a cyclist. A slight concussion subsequently produced headaches, a loss of memory, and a severe heart attack. In June of that year, Kraus was laid up for ten days. Two days before the end, in a moribund state, he blamed a doctor for his condition, but Helene Kann remonstrated with him: "Oh Karl, you are doing him an injustice, too!" Suddenly energized, Kraus sat up in bed and in a vigorous voice asked, "To whom have I ever done an injustice?!" [36] After two days of unconsciousness, an embolism caused Kraus's weakened heart to stop on June 12, 1936. In his testament, written on June 27 and 28, 1935, he asked his relatives to stay away from his interment, presumably because his life had, in deference to his work, not been much of a family affair. As Helene Kann recalls, "he used to say that he wanted to live forever ... the spirit ought to be powerful enough to prevent death." [37]

The publisher Kurt Wolff, who knew Kraus well, once remarked that there was always a kind of tension, whether of exaggerated love or exaggerated hatred, about him.[38] Erich Heller believes that "the satiric radicalism of Karl Kraus is only a defense mechanism of a man ardently in love with the beauty and joy of living." [39]

The meaning of this extremely productive life between love and hate is cogently expressed in two aphorisms and an epigram by Kraus. "Hate must make a man productive. Otherwise one might as well love" [40]; and "Ich war selten verliebt, immer verhasst." [41] (The play on words permits the translations "I have seldom been in love, always 'in hate'," or "... have always been hated.") The epigram runs as follows:

Der Unterschied

> Sie schienen schwer den Unterschied zu fassen,
> und aller Zwist war doch im Zweierlei:
> Ich gab mein Herz dahin im Hassen,
> Sie wussten nicht, was Liebe sei.[42]

(They seemed to have a hard time grasping the difference; and yet all contention lay in this duality: I gave my heart away in hating; they did not know what loving was.)

CHAPTER 2

The Torch

T HE THIRTY-SEVEN volumes of Kraus's periodical *Die Fackel (The Torch)* contain the major part of his literary output. In its impressive totality, *Die Fackel,* far from being a mere pillory, is not only a running autobiography but constitutes a unique history of Austrian culture and politics as well. It is also the source of most of Kraus's books. Kraus himself pointed out that what he wrote in his periodical should be regarded as advance printings of his books, and, with the exception of his poetry and *Literatur und Lüge (Literature and Lies,* 1929), those collections in book form which Kraus himself supervised were drawn from the *Fackel* up to 1918. Kraus bestowed infinite care upon his periodical and strove to make each issue a self-contained work of art. In addition to the very early writings, the only works that did not originally appear in the *Fackel* are his plays (excluding most of *Die letzten Tage der Menschheit*) and his adaptations of dramatic works by Nestroy, Shakespeare, and Offenbach. Kraus did not wish the *Fackel* up to issue No. 154 (February, 1904) to be considered as part of his collected works.

Die Fackel had two models. Kraus's direct inspiration was *Die Zukunft (The Future),* a periodical edited in Berlin by Maximilian Harden, whom Kraus admired and regarded as his mentor before he turned away from him and attacked him on literary as well as personal grounds. The indirect model was *La Lanterne,* a periodical that had appeared in Paris from 1868 to 1870 and had contained the writings of Henri Rochefort, an anti-Bonapartist writer who was politically oriented and, unlike Kraus, not primarily interested in language and culture. Kraus could not have called his magazine *Die Laterne* because of the word's polemical double meaning as something that gives light and may also serve for the hanging of aristocrats. Having been founded in 1899, *Die Fackel* originally appeared three times a month. Each issue—in small format and with striking red covers—contained from sixteen to twenty-four and later up to thirty-two pages. Robert Scheu's description of Vienna's reaction to the historic first issue of Kraus's periodical makes it plain that from April 1, 1899 on, Karl Kraus was a Viennese institution.

One day, as far as the eye could see, everything was—red. Vienna has not seen such a day since. What murmuring, whispering, spine-tingling! In the streets, on the streetcars, in the City Park, everyone was reading a red magazine. . . . Originally designed to flutter into the provinces in a few hundred copies, the little brochure had to be reprinted within a few days in tens of thousands of copies. And this whole issue, which was so chockful of wit that, as the *Arbeiterzeitung* put it, one had to read it carefully in order not to miss any of those glittering pearls, had been written by one man." [1]

Kraus soon smarted under "the accursed popularity which a grinning Vienna bestows" and noted that " 'Fackel-Kraus' is . . . the customary expression of an outlook on life which does not call the work after the man but the man after the merchandise." [2]

After 1904 the *Fackel* appeared "at irregular intervals," but at least four times a year. Subscriptions were valid not for a definite period of time but for a certain number of issues; after 1905 double and multiple issues were the rule rather than the exception, with the latter containing as many as 316 pages. The thirty-seven volumes consist of 415 different issues and 922 numbers. [3] Between 1899 and 1910 each volume ran to one thousand or eleven hundred pages; between 1911 and 1936, the average was six or seven hundred. About five thousand pages, one-fifth to one-sixth of the total contents of *Die Fackel,* were written by other contributors between 1899 and 1911. Thirty thousand copies of the first issue were sold, and by 1906 the circulation had stabilized at about nine thousand copies; but after 1911 it fluctuated between twenty-nine thousand and thirty-eight thousand. In Kraus's last years, the number of subscribers decreased to ten thousand or less. Starting with No. 263 (1908–9), *Die Fackel* also appeared in an edition printed especially for Germany.

Kraus's motto at the very beginning was not *"Was wir bringen"* ("What we shall print"), the announcement customarily made by a new publication, but *"Was wir umbringen"* ("What we shall destroy"). "May the *Fackel,*" the editor wrote in the very first issue, "provide light for a land in which, unlike the empire of Charles V, the sun never rises." [4]

Throughout its existence, *Die Fackel* lacked neither detractors nor imitators. In 1899 three issues of *Der Pinsel (The Brush* or *The*

Simpleton), a rather ineffective parodistic-polemical anti-*Fackel*, appeared under the editorship of Erwin Rosenberger, a Zionist journalist close to Theodor Herzl. *Der neue Simson (The New Samson)*, a crude dramatic satire by C. Karlweis (Karl Weiss), was performed in 1901. In June, 1901, following Annie Kalmar's death, Kraus took an extended vacation in Scandinavia. Upon his return to Vienna, he found that his printer, Moriz Frisch, had appointed his son as publisher of *Die Neue Fackel*. Kraus had to bring suit to restore his rights, but since Frisch had copyrighted the title page of the magazine in his own name, Kraus was no longer able to use the original cover drawing which showed a flaming torch. On October 4 of that year, Justinian Frisch put up posters proclaiming "*Die Fackel* is dead. Long live the *Neue Fackel*. Its publication date will be announced shortly." Later that month this plagiaristic publication, made up to look like Kraus's periodical, appeared under the title *Im Fackelschein (By Torchlight)*. While litigation was in progress, the title was changed to *Im Feuerschein,* but the ludicrously inept publication finally folded early in 1903. By that time Kraus's legal victory was complete, and from No. 82 (October, 1901) to the end, the *Fackel* was printed by the trusted firm of Jahoda & Siegel in the Verlag "Die Fackel," Vienna.[5]

The issue dated January, 1910, contains a complete list of contributors to the periodical. These included such distinguished writers and artists as Peter Altenberg, Richard Dehmel, Albert Ehrenstein, Egon Friedell, Paul Heyse, Oskar Kokoschka, Else Lasker-Schüler, Detlev von Liliencron, Adolf Loos, Samuel Lublinski, Heinrich Mann, Erich Mühsam, Arnold Schönberg, August Strindberg, Frank Wedekind, Franz Werfel, and Oscar Wilde—some fifty in all. Starting with No. 338 (December, 1911), however, Kraus was the sole contributor. "I no longer have any collaborators," he wrote. "I used to be envious of them. They repel those readers whom I want to lose myself." [6] For one thing, it gradually became too expensive for Kraus to pay writers of this caliber. Then, too, he applied the highest ethical standards to his writers; and because he expected of his contributors the strictest congruence of life and work, he was disappointed in all but a few of them. Quarrels among these and other authors arose because of intrigues, mounting personal ambition, and ingratitude toward Kraus. Given Kraus's technique of copious quotation, it may, of course, be argued that *Die Fackel* continued to have "contributors," if unwilling and unwitting ones, for the rest of its life. Being contained between the covers of the *Fackel* gave material that might have attracted little notice elsewhere a great deal of attention and a heightened relevance; for the *Fackel* had an unequalled satiric *genius loci:* "All of you know that the things you view with approbation elsewhere suddenly acquire another face here—by becoming what they are." [7]

Kraus repeatedly took pains to point out with pride that the *Fackel* was the only magazine in Austria which was not written to please its readers. With the exception of the early years, when some paid advertisements did appear (these ceased altogether in 1913), *Die Fackel* as a whole reflects an entirely uncommercial spirit. The following announcement, or some variant thereof, regularly appeared on its back cover: "It is requested that no books, periodicals, invitations, clippings, leaflets, manuscripts or written information of any sort be sent in. No such material will ever be returned, nor will any letters be answered. Any return postage that may be enclosed will be turned over to charity." And in 1921 Kraus wrote: "I read no manuscripts or leaflets, need no clippings, am interested in no journals, desire no review copies, nor do I send any out, review no books but throw them away, examine no talents, give no autographs, do not wish to be reviewed, mentioned, reprinted, propagated, disseminated, performed or recited; nor do I wish to be included in any catalogue, anthology or encyclopedia. . . ." [8]

Die Fackel did, however, include reviews of Kraus's writings and readings—more often than not from foreign sources. Although these should not be regarded as mere self-advertisement, they are undeniably attempts at self-justification. Kraus consistently made an effort to show the contrast between his international acceptance and the prophet's nonrecognition in his own country, in order to break through the wall of silence the Austrian press (with the partial exception of the Social Democratic *Arbeiterzeitung*) had erected around him and everything concerning him. In the same spirit, Kraus continued to print announcements of his own books as well as unpaid advertisements for the publications of writers he esteemed and wished to promote (Peter Altenberg, Else Lasker-Schüler, Georg Trakl, Liliencron, and Nestroy). In "Selbstbespiegelung" ("Spotlight on Myself"), a piece written in 1908, Kraus comes to terms with a reproach often leveled at him, that of egocentricity:

By speaking about myself, I, as a representative of Austrian cultural life, merely wish to forestall the danger of it being said some day that no one spoke about me in this country. . . . He who gladly does without the praise of the crowd will not deny himself an opportunity to be his own adherent.[9]

Kraus took the liberty to provide for himself all the amenities usually supplied to others by literary cliques. "No writer has ever made it easier for his readers to expose his vanity." [10] Indeed, he claimed special privileges for a new "publizistische Form", [11] a new kind of journalism.

"One of the most disagreeable concomitants of the *Fackel* is its readership," Kraus wrote. [12] "Antworten des Herausgebers" (replies by the editor) were a regular feature of the early years of the *Fackel*, being replaced by *Glossen* (from 1908 on), aphorisms (1906–17 and from 1919 on), [13] and epigrams (since 1916). In all of these forms Kraus attempted to come to terms with his readers, and despite the disclaimer cited above he wrote thousands of letters signed by the *Fackel* publishing house (Verlag der Fackel or Verlag "Die Fackel"). Certain of his posthumous fame and future relevance, Kraus, as early as 1932, mentioned a plan to publish a selection from these letters; but such a volume did not appear until 1962 with the customary complimentary close *"Mit vorzüglicher Hochachtung"* ("Respectfully Yours") as the somewhat ironic title.

"Most of the letters written in the *Fackel* publishing house do not at all refer to business," Kraus wrote and continued: "They are replies to correspondents whose approach was regarded as disgraceful—motivated cancellations of subscriptions if the subscriber, referring to this privilege, had dared come too close; reprimands to institutes which felt impelled to notify the publisher that they had entered a subscription; refusals of reprint rights which might have led to hateful attacks later on; notifications that no more free copies would be sent to editors who had gone beyond their privilege of reprinting the contents and had indulged in criticism; and the like." [14]

In a two-part essay entitled "Druck und Nachdruck" ("Print and Reprint," 1909–11), Kraus finds that the *Fackel*, having permitted reprints for a time, was often inaccurately quoted. From now on, he says, only piracy will be permitted: "Journalists are asked not to name the source they poison." [15]

In his book *The Hapsburg Monarchy*, published shortly before World War I, Henry Wickham Steed says of *Die Fackel*:

... a biting, stinging, sometimes scurrilous periodical pamphlet called the *Fackel*, which keeps a vigilant eye upon the follies and failings of daily journalism and pillories them mercilessly. The editor, proprietor and staff of the *Fackel* consist of one and the same person, Karl Kraus, a Jewish writer of remarkable talent. The daily press maintains a conspiracy of silence in regard to his very existence but he has nevertheless a faithful public of readers who enjoy his mordant satire and find in his brilliant style relief from the pomposities and bathos of Austrian journalese. . . . . He is an Ishmael, courting and requiting the hostility of his contemporaries but rarely allowing their shortcomings to pass unpunished. In one respect his efforts deserve specially honourable mention. He has encouraged by precept and practice the tendency of modern writers of German to react against the artificial clumsiness of the language and to prove that German can be written harmoniously.[16]

More recently, J. P. Stern has attempted to assess the uniqueness and significance of the *Fackel* by stating:

To delimit the intellectual region in which to place this journal, one would have to think of Péguy minus his Catholicism and patriotism; of F. R. Leavis uninvolved in any educational "establishment" plus genius; of the satirist in G. B. Shaw as milk-and-water to Kraus's vitriol; of the early Wittgenstein's equation of "language" and "world"; of H. L. Mencken's criticism of the leisure class; of the poet Siegfried Sassoon's "scarlet major at the base"; of the early Evelyn Waugh's satirical type-casting—and all this would have to be translated into the peculiar medium of Vienna.[17]

CHAPTER 3

K. K. versus Kakania

I *"Experiment Station for World Destruction"*

"WHEN A culture feels that its end has come, it sends for a priest." [1] With this statement Karl Kraus referred to the ossification of faith, the religious extremism and repressiveness which may be part of the rear-guard action of a period and a culture with an awareness that it is doomed. Although he regarded himself as a satirist *sui generis,* a unique and absolute phenomenon in the world of letters, Kraus clearly realized that he was a characteristic product of an *Endzeit* or *Spätzeit,* the late and final phase of an age or culture which has repeatedly produced great cultural critics and satirists.

When Kraus began to write, a century top-heavy with historical and cultural events and innovations was coming to an end. In the specific case of his homeland, which was both the source and the target of his satire, the Habsburg dynasty (worn out after a reign of some six hundred years) was coming to an end, and so was Austria-Hungary, the political constellation of the last fifty years. The reign of Emperor Franz Joseph spanned almost seven decades and witnessed the slow, inevitable dissolution of an age-old political, social, and cultural structure. Kraus began to write at a turning point in history, at a time of overrefinement and overripeness to the point of decay and death. His marked apocalyptic sense and stance as a "late" warner derive from his epoch's *Zeitgeist*—impermanence, transitoriness, disintegration—,from its *Lebensgefühl* of melancholia and inner insecurity. Many of Kraus's literary contemporaries regarded themselves as effete heirs of a highly developed but irrevocably declining tradition and culture. "Not only Vienna's finest writers," wrote Carl Schorske, "but her painters and psychologists, even her art historians, were preoccupied with the problem of the individual in a disintegrating society." [2] While the main literary movement in Germany at the end of the century was a socially conscious, economically oriented, politically aware Naturalism, the Austrian poets of the *fin de siècle* did not participate in any activist movement, but instead strove to preserve their tradition and cope with reality or screen it out in symbolistic and impressionistic ways.

From 1867, the date of the *Ausgleich* or Compromise with Hungary, until the end of World War I in 1918, Vienna was the "Imperial-Royal Capital City" of the Dual Monarchy of Austria and Hungary. The empire's population of approximately fifty million comprised some twelve million German-speaking Austrians, about ten million Hungarians and five million Poles, as well as Czechs, Slovaks, Rumanians, Slovenes, Croats, Serbs, Ukrainians, Italians, Jews, and gypsies. Far from being a unified entity, this mixture of peoples produced constant clashes and conflicts of an ethnic, political, economic, and social nature. Yet the dying decades of Austria's cosmopolitan culture produced a remarkable cultural flowering even as the country was on the downward slope politically and socially—a *"farbenvoller Untergang"* or colorful sunset, as the German poet Stefan George put it.[3] Among the natives or residents of Kraus's Austria whose creativity has been influential far beyond the confines of their country and their time may be mentioned the artists Oskar Kokoschka, Gustav Klimt, and Egon Schiele; the composers Anton Bruckner, Gustav Mahler, Hugo Wolf, Arnold Schönberg, and Alban Berg; the philosophers and natural scientists Moritz Schlick, Ernst Mach, Ludwig Wittgenstein, Christian von Ehrenfels, and Rudolf Carnap; the physicians and psychiatrists Theodor Billroth, Julius von Wagner-Jauregg, Julius Tandler, Karl Landsteiner, Sigmund Freud, Alfred Adler, Richard von Krafft-Ebing, and Theodor Reik; the economists Karl Menger and Joseph Schumpeter; the architects Otto Wagner and Adolf Loos; Bertha von Suttner and Alfred H. Fried, the indefatigable fighters for peace; and Theodor Herzl, the father of political Zionism.

In his monumental novel *Der Mann ohne Eigenschaften (The Man Without Qualities),* Robert Musil deals with the declining decades of his native country, which he calls "Kakanien" (Kakania). This is an inspired reference to the magical and mysterious letters "K.K." (pronounced "kah kah" in German), which stood for *"kaiserlich-königlich"* (imperial-royal) and served to designate the offices, institutions, and titles of the Austrian part of the Dual Monarchy. (K. u. K., imperial *and* royal, referred to joint institutions, such as the foreign ministry and the army, but these distinctions were unclear or became blurred in practice, causing Kakanian confusion.) As Musil put it,

The administration of this country was carried out in an enlightened, hardly perceptible manner, with a cautious clipping of all sharp points, by the best bureaucracy in Europe, which could be accused of only one defect: it could not help regarding genius and enterprise of genius in private persons, unless privileged by high birth or State appointment, as ostentation, indeed presumption. But who would want unqualified persons putting their oar in, anyway? And besides, in Kakania it was only that a genius was always regarded as a lout, but never, as sometimes happened elsewhere, that a mere lout was regarded as a genius. . . . Those national struggles . . . were so violent that they several times a year caused the machinery of State to jam and come to a dead stop. But between whiles, in the breathing-spaces between government and government, everyone got on excellently with everyone else and behaved as though nothing had ever been the matter. Nor had anything real ever been the matter. It was nothing more than the fact that every human being's dislike of every other human being's attempts to get on—a dislike in which today we are all agreed—in that country crystallized earlier, assuming the form of a sublimated ceremonial that might have become of great importance if its evolution had not been prematurely cut short by a catastrophe. . . . Yes, in spite of much that seems to point the other way, Kakania was perhaps a home for genius after all; and that, probably, was the ruin of it.[4]

Karl Kraus shared his initials with Imperial-Royal Austria, a state which he attacked with greater consistency and vehemence than any other writer of his time. By virtue of its strategic position in Central Europe and the unique blend of its culture, Austria had long been regarded as a Europe *in nuce,* as a proving ground for Europe and, indeed, the world. To this old insight Karl Kraus characteristically added a new satiric note by calling Austria a *"Versuchsstation für Weltuntergang"* [5], an experiment station for world destruction. His prewar writings constitute variations on this major theme, pillorying numerous aspects of Austria and Austrian society, whose activities Kraus viewed as one vast rehearsal for doom. These attacks reached their climax in wartime. In a poem entitled "Nach zwanzig Jahren" ("After Twenty Years"), Kraus expressed his relief at no longer having even a verbal connection with the hated political structure:

> Ich atme auf, die lästige Begleitung,
> das andere K.K., der *nom de guerre,*
> der Schatten meines wahren Namens wich
> mir von der Seite in das Schattenreich . . .
> Mein Wort hat Österreich-Ungarn überlebt.[6]

(I breathe a sigh of relief. That burdensome companion, the other K.K., the *nom de guerre,* the shadow of my true name, left my side and went to the realm of the dead. . . . My words have outlived Austria-Hungary.)

II   The Demolished Literature

Kraus's first major satirical work was a literary satire entitled *Die demolirte Literatur (The Demolished Literature),* which first appeared in the *Wiener Rundschau* in 1896. It was published as a pamphlet in the following year and achieved five editions by 1901. Although it presupposed a good acquaintance with contemporary literature and literary cliques, this witty diatribe, so rich in innuendo and invective, was widely noticed and netted its author at least one challenge to a duel and one bodily attack. Karl Kraus later disowned it, refused to have it reprinted, and expressed his conviction that one line in the *Fackel* outweighed all such writings artistically.

Kraus starts with the memorable line "Wien wird jetzt zur Grosstadt demoliert" [7] ("Vienna is now being demolished into a metropolis"). The essay is actually an obituary of the Café Griensteidl, one of the most memorable segments of old Vienna's coffee-house culture. Now that this building is being torn down, Kraus reasons, our literature is left without a shelter, for in this comfortable if drafty place even the waiters had literary pretensions and adapted themselves to changing currents like Naturalism and Symbolism. With the great exodus impending, the poets—truly a motley crew—hastily pack their literary paraphernalia, such as lack of talent, premature detachment, poses, megalomania, girls from the outlying districts, cravats, hothouse moods, mannerisms, monocles, misused datives, and secret nerves.

The Café Griensteidl had been the favorite gathereing place of the "Young Vienna" circle of poets, and, without mentioning them by name, Kraus satirizes most of them—the one notable exception being Peter Altenberg, to whom he felt close. With the exception of Hermann Bahr, the "gentleman from Linz" who is depicted on the cover as being dragged off by two attendants, Kraus's attitude toward all these writers was an ambivalent one. These "aristocratic poets whose nobility already encompasses several degenerations" [8] seem to have chosen dying as their main theme. In these "Jung-Wien" writers Kraus diagnosed a curious inbreeding and inactivity, a narrow horizon and great shallowness. Arthur Schnitzler is treated relatively gently as the man "who has plunged deepest into this shallowness and is most deeply immersed in this emptiness" [9], and who has put suburban girls on the stage of the Burgtheater (as the figure of *"das süsse Mädel"*). The other writers whose penchants and peculiarities are mercilessly satirized are more or less easily identified; they include major figures such as Felix Salten, Richard Beer-Hofmann (a poet who writes sparingly and is a clothes horse and an *arbiter elegantiarum*), and Leopold von Andrian-Werberg, as well as minor writers like Felix Dörmann, the librettist Viktor Leon (Hirschfeld), and the painter-poet Ferry Beraton.

The one member of this group whom Kraus was to attack for the rest of his life was Hermann Bahr.[10] Kraus regarded him as a literary and cultural chameleon who "overcame" one *-ism* after another. Bahr affected the "Linz custom of indicating genius by having a lock of hair hanging down over one's forehead." [11] His Storm and Stress years have now given way to Olympian detachment à la Goethe. Generally a tireless champion of mediocrities—or so Kraus regarded him—,Bahr did make one major discovery: the incredibly precocious Hugo von Hofmannsthal, whom he described as "Goethe on a school bench." [12] Kraus was later to make this unkind remark about Hofmannsthal: "Miracle of nature! The artificial flowers of Herr von Hofmannsthal, which had dew around 1895, are now withered." [13] In another context, Kraus described Hofmannsthal, whose poetic well appeared to have run dry, as "long since sober rather than intoxicated by golden goblets in which there is no wine." [14] Now that this "literature" is being "demolished" and the poets are being evicted, Kraus feels that "life will break the crutches of affectation." [15] Yet they must have a gathering place; what, Kraus wonders, will be their future Griensteidl?

III   A Crown for Zion

Kraus wrote the twenty-eight-page pamphlet entitled *Eine Krone für Zion (A Crown for Zion)* at Ischl in September, 1898; its third printing in the following year roughly coincided with his leaving the Jewish fold. Although of minor importance in Kraus's total output, this somewhat superficial essay remains a significant document in Kraus's forty-year war against part of his own self, his roots, and certain aspects of his own intellectuality; for in it he attempts to come to terms with political Zionism, a new movement which was posing an intellectual, economic, social, and personal challenge to Jews and non-Jews alike.

The title of Kraus's work puns on the dual meaning of the word *Krone:* a royal or imperial crown, and the monetary unit of the time. Kraus had been asked to contribute a *shekel* (in the amount of one crown) for "those purposes which they call Zionist or, to use a good old word, anti-Semitic." [16] In fact, the bulletin announcing the First Zionist Congress had actually listed Kraus as a delegate. Kraus contributed his shekel since he believed that the disappointed Polish proletarians would benefit materially after the Zionist movement had failed. In 1897 he had written an unfavorable review (in *Die Wage*) of Theodor Herzl's *The New Ghetto,* "a play which presents an altogether corrupt Jewish society, but disappoints with its unexpected emphasis on one noble-minded Israelite, which cost the author the sympathies of authoritative anti-Semitic circles." [17]

Political Zionism, the movement founded by Herzl, a fellow journalist and cultural editor of the *Neue Freie Presse,* was viewed by Kraus as something artificial and divisive. The key to his negative attitude was the young Kraus's belief in assimilation and in socialism. While he did not doubt that something had to be done for the endangered Jewish masses in Eastern Europe, he felt that Western Jews needed no such movement, and that a sort of oriental enclave in Western culture was an abomination. Kraus felt that only socialism—and not Zionism, which he regarded as a Western bourgeois movement—could rescue Eastern Jewry. According to him, the assimilated Jews were living peacefully and contentedly in the West, and only their lack of political skill was erecting artificial dividing walls. It was "dark orthodoxy" that prevented the countries in which there was real suffering from acknowledging the international proletarian misery. "And now hundreds of thousands who are waiting to be redeemed by joining universal human misery are being held fast in Jewish misery which offers no prospects for the future." [18]

Kraus makes satirical remarks on the First Zionist Congress, which had taken place at Basle in 1897, on the basis of its official minutes and reports. He ridicules the exclusive concentration of the delegates on Jewish national promises and tasks and lampoons their pathos and emotionalism. The sole purpose of the congress seems to have been to rally round the Star of David: "It took narrow-minded Zionism, whose political line can easily be followed to the nearby point of real impossibility, to enable these gentlemen, who have hitherto been occupied only with their nerves, to feel that they too are of this day and age." [19] With astonishing speed they have absorbed the millennial pain of Jewry, and this enables them to assume undreamt-of new poses and abandon their coffee-house estheticism.

Kraus professes to be amused by the coming transition from the perfume-laden atmosphere of bourgeois salons to agricultural schemes. Belletristic bon vivants are to become Assyrians, a Viennese *süsses Mädel* is to turn into a Miriam, and their national idol will henceforth be called Hermann Bar-Kochba. Calling Herzl "the King of Zion," [20] Kraus lampoons attempts to create a Jewish national culture with

Jewish heroes. He would rather turn things around. "The most refractory Zionist could easily be civilized and turned into a European in but a few years." [21] The "faith of the fathers," the best orthodoxy, ought to be an unshakable belief in the adaptability of the Jewish character, for the Jews are "destined to merge indissolubly with all surrounding cultures and yet constantly to remain a ferment," and "where a down-to-earth settlement project is involved, messianic rapture is entirely dispensable." [22]

Kraus feels that Zionism fosters anti-Semitism. These Jews-at-any-price emphasize their Jewish physical "stigmata," so that it is now meritorious to have a hooked nose. Kraus believed that vulgar anti-Semitism would have vanished without this new provocation. The Pan-Germans, he points out, have their hands full with the Slavs and the Clericals and would have left the Jewish question in abeyance. And when it comes to practical organization rather than theoretical vaporings, insuperable difficulties present themselves. The view of the "land of milk and honey" is a naïve one. Kraus foresees linguistic problems as well, and asks: "Is the belief in Dr. Herzl's talent as an essayist so strong that he will be able to form a state transcending all linguistic differences?" [23]

Far from conceding that the Jews are, in Herzl's phrase, "a people, one people," Kraus calls them a "decaying people." [24] He considers "playing at nations" about as durable and long-lived a game as the nineteenth century. "When Zionists share a rather skimpy *Weltanschauung* with anti-Semites, it must soon be exhausted." [25] Kraus says that he is almost ashamed to furnish emphatic opposition to such a feeble, shallow movement. Nor does he wish to be the spokesman of arrogant, highly placed Jews who ape Gentiles and look down their noses at their more lowly coreligionists. "The production of a *fata morgana* is not a social reform but a false pretense," [26] he writes. "One can hardly assume that this time the Jews will enter the Promised Land with dry feet; another Red Sea, Socialism, will block their way there. . . . Come unto me, all ye that labor and are laden. Do not let yourselves be depressed by the Zionist promises of a better future." [27]

Not content with attacking Zionism, Kraus also impugns the motives of the Zionist leaders, "sensitive souls made blasé by early successes, which their talent and luck brought them in great profusion; now they need a new, more serious substance for their lives." [28] He claims that Herzl needed the transition from the cultural page to the editorial page and ends with a dig at Max Nordau, that "great literary doctor" and chairman of the Zionist Congress. From these statements it is obvious that Kraus was attacking Herzl not so much as the father of political Zionism but as a staff member of the hated *Neue Freie Presse* who continued to work for a paper which steadfastly ignored the great idea of his life and the movement which he had started. It is curious, incidentally, that Herzl did not mention Kraus and his pamphlet in his voluminous *Diaries* which, from 1895 to his death in 1904, were entirely devoted to "the Jewish Cause." [29] While some of Kraus's arguments were not much different from the strictures and gibes frequently encountered by Herzl, his early prominence, his connection with the *Neue Freie Presse,* and his style surely made his attack worthy of Herzl's attention.

Kraus proved to be a poor prophet on the Jewish question. In later years, he did abandon some of his earlier positions, though he never really disavowed *A Crown for Zion.* He did not issue a "manifesto of contempt" [30] for it, but in a piece entitled "Ich bekenne" ("I Confess")[31] he said that he would now present most of the material in his pamphlet differently or not at all. By that time (1924) Kraus had read Herzl's Diaries, which had appeared in the early 1920s, and had changed his mind about Herzl's personal probity and his manful struggle against great odds. That he had had second thoughts on Zionism as well is evidenced by a statement he made in 1913: "Jewish nationalism is to be welcomed, like any step back from a pseudonymous culture to a point where its substance is once more worthy of being a problem." [32]

Kraus's attitude toward Judaism and Jewishness can only be sketched here briefly, yet it is of great importance in his life and his work. As a satirist he has been called everything from "a shining example of Jewish self-hatred" [33] to "an Old Testament prophet who pours cataracts of wrath over his people" [34] and "an arch-Jew." [35] Kraus did not have an analytical mind but one that was characterized by intuitive flashes of wit and insight; on the basis of his writings there is some justification for all of the above designations. In his works, there is virtually no discussion of Jewish religion or ethics; to him the Jews were an ethnic or social group, and he had an aversion to being considered part of *any* group. In 1914 he identified *"Gemütlichkeit* and Jewishness" as "the driving forces of Austrian decay," [36] and earlier he had defined a Viennese as "this cross between a Viennese and a Jew, that unclear solution of a racial problem." [37]

Just as Kraus regarded himself as the very antipode of the Viennese brand of *Gemütlichkeit,* which denoted moral and emotional laxity and political immaturity to him, and just as his own absolute commitment and his crystalline style were in conflict with his environment and his time, so he strove to overcome what he regarded as the negative element of his Jewish heritage. Leopold Liegler, a man not otherwise in sympathy with the Jewish spirit, concedes that "the extreme ethical orientation of his personality can certainly be associated with what is specifically Jewish in him" and goes on to say that Kraus has made "the most radical break which a man can make: the break with Judaism." [38] Liegler describes Kraus as "a man with the intellectual and linguistic power of the great prophets who has traversed the road from Judaism to freedom." [39] According to him, Kraus saw in the Jewish problem the turning point of his own development and, above all, the nucleus and source of the general process of cultural deterioration.

Theodor Lessing included "the boundless moral zealot" [40] Kraus in his classic study *Jüdischer Selbsthass,* pointing out that Kraus embodied the self-hatred of ethically motivated persons in a particularly tragic form. "The fact that Kraus was Jewish," writes Frank Field, "is of vital importance in understanding the particular extremism, the *Angst,* the sense of the apocalyptic which pervades his work." [41] Field believes that Kraus was and remained intensely Jewish, and he places him in the tradition of that "masochistic antisemitism" [42] which was a characteristic feature of many German and Austrian Jews. Like Gustav Mahler, Kraus was full of contradictions: "A Jew who had renounced Judaism and yet, for that very reason, felt even more acutely Jewish than before." [43]

Kraus's lifelong fight against the press cannot be sundered from the fact that his most telling invectives were directed against the largely Jewish-owned and Jewish-staffed liberal newspapers. ("As compared to the Jewish press, the anti-Semitic press owes the fact that it is less dangerous to its more pronounced lack of talent.") [44] Kraus felt that the Jewish press was better at creating anti-Semitism than at combating it. In his view, the Jews' obstinate clinging to religious and ethnic customs produced a latent feeling of alienation which, from time to time, flared up into virulent race hatred and persecution. Kraus's repeated excoriation of the worldwide Jewish feeling of solidarity explains his curious stand on the Dreyfus affair. In 1899 he printed in the *Fackel* a series of articles by Wilhelm Liebknecht, the grand old man of German socialism, in opposition to pro-Jewish and anti-French agitation; he apparently feared that such agitation could only freeze positions and heighten nationalism and militarism.

Viewed in the context of Kraus's numerous other opinions and polemics, his attitude in the Dreyfus affair was probably not another instance of Jewish anti-Semitism, but was presumably based on the feeling that, given Austria's numerous internal problems, no interference in a military controversy of another state was advisable. In December, 1915, Kraus reprinted Dostoevsky's essay on the Jewish question, which focuses on the motif of the feeling of strangeness created by the Jews. Soon thereafter he wrote "Gebet an die Sonne von Gibeon" ("Prayer to the Sun of Gibeon"),[45] a lengthy ode full of prophetic pathos in which he not only lashes out at the nationalistic megalomania of the Book of Joshua,[46] but curses the Judaization of Germanic culture, the Jews' ruthless pursuit of material power in concert with the Germans, and their belief that they are the Chosen People; Jews have spread the poison of money and thus reduced all potentates and peoples to slaves.

Field believes that Kraus "attacked his own people in the same way that the prophets of the Old Testament had castigated the unworthiness of the Israelites for the trust which God had placed in them."[47] This view is supported by one of Kraus's own statements: "I believe I can say about myself that I go along with the development of Judaism up to the Exodus, but that I don't participate in the dance around the Golden Calf and, from that point on, share only in those characteristics which were also found in the defenders of God and in the avengers of a people gone astray."[48] This statement was made in 1913 in response to a letter from a reader who had asked Kraus whether he believed he had none of the commonly noticed Jewish characteristics and what he thought of the statement, à la Dr. J. Lanz von Liebenfels, that a man cannot secede from his race.

Unlike that curious pseudo-scientist, who had hailed Kraus as the savior of the *Ariogermanen,* the benefactor of the "Aryan Germanic" spirit,[49] Kraus denied being an expert on race, but expressed his belief that he had none of the qualities deemed Jewish at present. Kraus pointed out that he had never denied his Jewish background so as to be able to consort with officers, counts, and prelates; nor had he ever written or done anything designed to ingratiate himself with the garden variety of vulgar anti-Semites.

I don't know whether it is a Jewish quality to deem the Book of Job as worth reading, or whether it is anti-Semitism to throw a book by Schnitzler into a corner, whether it is Jewish or German to feel that the writings of the Jews Else Lasker-Schüler and Peter Altenberg are closer to God and to language than anything that German literature has produced in the last fifty years.[50]

Nor did he know whether it was a Jewish quality "to regard an old purveyor of schnapps who wears a kaftan as a higher form of culture than a member of an Austrian writers' association dressed in a tuxedo."[51]

Such statements, to be sure, must be balanced against numerous phrases which one would expect to find only in the pages of vicious Jew-baiting journals like *Der Stürmer* ("Jew boys are the poets of a nation to which they do not belong";[52] "the inevitable pogrom of the Jews against ideals";[53] "a state which has the most corrupt Jewish influences circulating in its veins";[54] "the destruction of Austria by Jerusalem.")[55] Kraus rarely missed an opportunity to inveigh against Jewish stock exchange speculators, industrial magnates, and financial tycoons. Jewish cliquishness and solidarity were anathema to him. "The Jews live in an inbreeding of humor," he once wrote. "When among themselves, it is all right for them to poke fun at one another. But woe if they should separate."[56] Equally disarming is Kraus's definition of anti-Semitism as "that frame of mind which musters and means seriously about one-tenth of the reproaches which stock exchange humorists hold in readiness for their own kind."[57]

Some of Kraus's most rousing polemics were conducted against Jews: Moriz Benedikt, the head of the *Neue Freie Presse;* the journalists Maximilian Harden and Imre Békessy; and the critic Alfred Kerr. Yet, in the tradition of anti-Semites, Gentile or Jewish, it may be said of Kraus that some of his best friends were Jews; among them the writers Peter Altenberg, Franz Janowitz, and Otto Weininger; the publisher Kurt Wolff, the printer Georg Jahoda, and the bookdealer Richard Lanyi; the musicians Franz Mittler, Otto Janowitz, and Georg Knepler; the theater men and writers Berthold Viertel and Heinrich Fischer; and the attorney Oskar Samek. It may be symptomatic, too, that most of the major books and essays on Kraus that have appeared during the past decade or so were written by Jews: Werner Kraft, Hans Kohn, Hans Weigel, Wilma Iggers, Erich Heller, J. P. Stern, Paul Engelmann, Paul Hatvani, and the author of the present study.

Kraus's convoluted Jewishness is a controversial and ambivalent matter that may be illuminated by paraphrasing Talleyrand's well-known dictum about war: Kraus may have felt that anti-Semitism was too important a matter to be entrusted to anti-Semites.

IV   Morality and Criminal Justice

The early Kraus was a casuist, that is, he applied broad ethical concepts, precepts, and standards to specific situations and supplied massive evidence of the corruption rampant in Austrian public life. But gradually he strove to transcend specific cases and occasions and to develop a more universally valid cultural criticism.

In *Sittlichkeit and Kriminalität,* a book which appeared in 1908 and contains forty-one articles from *Die Fackel*–ranging from 1902, the date of the title essay, to 1907–Kraus was concerned with morality as it was manifested in Austria's courtrooms and newspapers in the early years of this century; and yet its accurate description of human nature makes it a timeless document. The title, translated literally as "Morality and Criminality," really means "Morality and Criminal Justice" or "Court Justice," since Kraus was intent upon laying bare the contrast between private and public morality and showing the hypocrisy inherent in the administration of Austrian justice. "As long as Austrian criminal laws are in force, one won't know what hurts more–the false interpretation of a serviceable clause or the correct application of an unserviceable one." [58]

With these sharp satirical pieces Kraus mounts an attack on the hypocrisy of a male society which condemns by day what it enjoys by night. Kraus lashes out at the narrowness of hidebound judges who are out of touch with reality and of jurors of substandard intelligence and a business mentality. Again and again he castigates the distorted, sensational newspaper reports which, to his mind, are more immoral than the crime itself. The book is one long elaboration of the basic Krausian insight that sexual scandal begins when the police put a stop to it.

Kraus saw a direct line from individual to general immorality and pointed out that in a trial of this sort the proven guilt of the defendant stood out luminously from the gloomy background of general immorality. For Kraus, justice could and should achieve only the protection of property, of defenseless and under-age persons, and of health; this, he felt, could be accomplished without encroaching upon the private sphere. He believed that what two adults did of their own free will and within their own walls was their affair and not legally actionable. While trying to combat Austria's "open season" on women, Kraus, curiously enough, did not really approve of women's rights except in the sexual sphere.

In Kraus's development, this collection marked a progression from journalist to polemicist to moralist and the transformation of a critic of society into a critic of culture. The first five volumes of the *Fackel* had been relatively tame, but now there appeared a new polemical vehemence, yet one coupled with great compassion and chivalry, and a new sense of ethical mission directed at the universal—even though, characteristically, the events, circumstances, and persons triggering the satire were local, either Viennese or Austrian.

With the essays in *Sittlichkeit und Kriminalität,* Kraus attempted to establish ethical order in a period of transition from the nineteenth to the twentieth century, when eroticism and sexuality fairly flooded European literature and culture—as witness the works of Strindberg, Zola, Wedekind, Flaubert, Wilde, Weininger, and Freud. Kraus was not so much interested in sexuality as in eroticism; he regarded the latter as a great inspirer of, and source for, artists. "Eroticism is to sexuality as gain is to loss," he wrote.[59] He felt that the very wellsprings of life—love and beauty—had been sullied and stopped up for many years. As in so many things, Kraus was eclectic in accepting or rejecting new ideas and insights in this field; he used whatever elements seemed necessary to him for self-liberation and for sounding a clarion call for naturalness in human values. For example, when Otto Weininger's controversial book *Geschlecht und Charakter (Sex and Character)* appeared in 1903, Kraus wrote to the author: "An admirer of women enthusiastically agrees with the arguments of your contempt for women." [60] Kraus had come to different conclusions from Weininger's premises, his "sexual types" and his differentiation between the male and female principle. He equally appreciated the "demonic woman" of Weininger and Strindberg and the instinctual, ingenuous "child-woman" of the German dramatist Frank Wedekind. In May, 1905, when Wedekind was bedeviled by censorship because of his daring sexual themes, Kraus arranged the first Vienna performances of his play *Die Büchse der Pandora* and even took a small part in it.[61] Wedekind had written in the Foreword to his drama:

The tragic central figure of this play is not Lulu . . . but Countess Geschwitz . . . a human being burdened with the curse of abnormality. . . . It is a matter of fact that the chief protagonists in the old Greek tragedies are almost always beyond the pale of normality. They are of the race of Tantalus; the gods have forged an iron band around their brows.[62]

Kraus attempted to remove this iron band from the brow of every woman, be she princess or prostitute, and attacked with all the verbal resources at his comand the men—anything but gods—who had forged it. He believed that it was the essential nature of woman to give in to the stirrings of her sexuality and that it was a crime against nature to place female sexuality in the straitjacket of moral responsibility. The viewpoint expressed in these essays was one that never changed during Kraus's long career, just as justice never changed in trying to entrap defenseless women and homosexuals. Those who live by their instincts were defended by him no matter how lowly their station in life may have been, for the depravity of their enemies gave them dignity and a raison d'être.

The book begins with seven brief quotations from *King Lear* and *Measure for Measure;* these passages, to Kraus, contained the last word on the morals which gave rise to *Ehebruchsprozess P.,* a double trial for adultery which was shamefully conducted in a courtroom in the summer of 1901—"a St. Vitus's Dance of Justice"[63]—and woefully reported by the press. "Culture is where the laws of the state are Shakespearean thoughts in the form of legal sections," [64] where the leaders keep Shakespeare in mind when they act. "An adultery trial," Kraus writes, "is the great opportunity to demonstrate the incompatibility between morality and court justice." [65] Criminal justice does not have anything to do with "morality"; only local gossip does. A legislator should not appear in the role of a snooping reporter.

In this trial, the defendant told how a matchmaker's services had been enlisted before marriage and how she had committed adultery after being mistreated and abused. A good judge, Kraus points out, would have recognized mitigating circumstances and given her a light sentence, forestalling the sensationalism that poisoned the moral atmosphere of a great city for weeks. He referred to "tortures that were not known in the Middle Ages, which knew only thumb screws, not the *press.*" [66] Pointing out that German philosophers have always advocated an easier divorce for women, Kraus believed that marriage would be a far more sacred institution if wives ceased to become "legal property." [67] But a self-styled "infallible" judge, unfairly on the side of the plaintiff, seemed to subject only the woman to laws of morality, insulting, humiliating, and pillorying her at every turn. Even after confessions had been made, the judge cited the defendants' love letters in court. Kraus lashes out at a mentality which approves of marrying for money and frowns on sex-for-sale, which turns a wife into a prostitute and values a loved wife less than an unloved one.

In instance after instance, Kraus is concerned with major and minor miscarriages of justice—the little tragedies of jurisprudence as they are publicly reflected—,detailing the cat-and-mouse game which prosecutors play with the prosecuted and fastening on absurdities and ambiguities in the law and on the duplicity of its representatives. The judges of morality let the ravens get away with anything while they condemn and punish the doves. A man who tried to steal a kiss was sentenced to four months in jail, while a woman who repeatedly and unmercifully beat her three-year-old child was let off with a reprimand.

"Die Hetzjagd auf das Weib" ("Open Season on Women") is concerned with the "guiltless guilt" of a beautiful woman whom men seem bent upon defaming.[68] In "Die Presse als Kupplerin" ("The Pandering Press")[69] and "Eros und Themis"[70] Kraus is concerned with journalists who condemn immorality on the editorial page while their advertising department takes money for dubious advertisements; Themis, the personification of justice, seems to play blind man's bluff with Eros. The same issue of the *Neue Freie Presse* in which sexual perverseness was decried ran ads of "masseuses" named Hedwig Faust (Fist), Wanda Stock (Stick), Paula Ruthner (Rodner), Carola Prügler (Whipper), Wanda Schläger (Beater), and Minna Beinhacker (Leg-chopper).

Kraus rates Johann Feigl, the deputy presiding justice of the Vienna District Court, as an *"Unhold,"* a monster in judicial robes, because he gave a life sentence to a twenty-three-year-old purse snatcher who had stood up and talked back to him. Kraus suggests that the confession of Feigl's greatest sin would be "I have spent a lifetime applying the Austrian Criminal Code."[71] In "Irrenhaus Österreich"[72] ("Insane Asylum Austria"), Kraus speaks of the humbug of "psychiatromania" and wonders, apropos of the case of Princess Louise of Coburg, whether psychiatrists sometimes render judgments of sanity or insanity for tendentious or political reasons; for even such eminent men as Wagner-Jauregg and Krafft-Ebing have sometimes lent their names to psychiatric-legal abominations and forensic fallacies.

In "Der Hexenprozess von Leoben," Kraus skillfully quotes from the history of German culture and mores to show parallels between old witches' trials and a modern one. He states, "The technique of a witches' trial has been strikingly perfected by the invention of journalistic black magic."[73] Far from fearing the publicity their depravity might receive, the judges at such a trial use this publicity to increase the torment of their victims. At the very bottom of Austrian popular consciousness there lurks the desire to see some devils exorcised. In this case, the authorities had to search for the deed rather than the culprit. "Verbrecher gesucht" ("Criminals Wanted") is couched in a similar vein. Kraus quotes Oscar Wilde: "The less punishment, the less crime." [74] But Austria believes in the power of the state as an end in itself; the people are regarded as an institution intended to serve the officials, who could do their jobs more easily if there were no people. Sometimes the police know that a crime is going to be committed, but no action is taken.

In "Der Meldzettel" ("The Registration Form"), Kraus satirizes arch-bureaucracy and the invasion of privacy. In the vein of De Quincey's "Murder Considered as One of the Fine Arts," Kraus writes: "Unfortunately it is not beyond the realm of possibility that the criminals who have already committed theft, fraud, robbery and murder will risk also the ultimate and most horrible of all crimes: false registration." [75]

"Die Kinderfreunde" ("The Friends of Children") deals with the trial of Professor Theodor Beer who was accused of having taken two boys to his photographic library, shown them obscene pictures, and made them masturbate. Dr. Beer was sentenced to three months in jail for homosexuality, not for corrupting the morals of a minor. "Who harmed the poor boys more," asks Kraus, "the photographer who undressed them in his studio or the fathers who undressed them in the courtroom?" [76] Their "friends" placed the boys in the lion's maw of big-city sensationalism, increasing the psychic damage a hundredfold and stoking the fires of prurience, perverseness, and publicity. Viennese parents went to great lengths to prove that Dr. Beer had corrupted their children as well; the half-understood statements of children were eagerly used to destroy a man's reputation and his very existence. The fate of the two boys seems less harsh to Kraus than the fate of child laborers, exploited children, and animals forced to pull great loads; and the Beer trial is yet another instance of justice digging far deeper into the private life of an accused person than is warranted by his deed.

A number of the cases detailed in *Sittlichkeit und Kriminalität* involve prostitution, and since the physical prostitution of women seemed far less deleterious to Kraus than the intellectual prostitution of men, this gave him an opportunity to comment on the keyhole peeping and the self-righteous hypocrisy of Austrian society. "Corruption is worse than prostitution," he wrote in November, 1904; "the latter might endanger the morals of an individual, the former invariably endangers the morals of the entire community." [77]

"Die Kussräuberin" [78] deals with an eighteen-year-old prostitute who was jailed for two weeks because she had given someone a kiss at a railroad station. "Der Fall Riehl" ("The Riehl Case," November, 1906)[79] concerns the trial of a madam named Regine Riehl who was accused of exploiting her girls economically and ruining their health. In Kraus's view, the persecution of pandering can only promote such exploitation. "Squeeze human nature into the straitjacket of criminal justice and crime will appear!" [80] Blackmail flourishes when the state and society relegate sexual intercourse to the dark area of disreputable silence. The very word *"Schandlohn"* (wages of shame) is symptomatic. To despise a woman who sells her body is to despise the principles of logic. Feminists fight for the political emancipation of women but neglect their sexual emancipation. Approved institutions, such as an unhappy marriage or a reputable but repressive educational establishment like a parochial boarding school, often do more to stunt a woman's sound sexual instincts than sexual license could: "Morality is a venereal disease. Its primary stage is called virtue; its secondary stage, boredom; its tertiary stage, syphilis." [81]

In "Rund um den Schandlohn," [82] Kraus quotes a statement made at the Munich Congress to Combat White Slavery to the effect that the patrons of bordellos ought to pay the inmates badly so as to make the girls think twice before attaching themselves to such establishments! A Christian-Socialist paper having demanded that prostitution be divested of its esthetic attractiveness and made plain and unappealing, the police removed the piano from the salon of a bordello. For a prostitute to be licensed, Kraus points out in "Die Ära nach dem Prozess Riehl" ("The Post-Riehl Era"), her "total moral depravity" [83] has to be demonstrated. To furnish such proof, a woman would have to be encouraged to practice a little illicit, clandestine prostitution first! Actually, it is made very difficult for a prostitute to mend her ways and return to a more respectable existence; for these women are duped and entrapped at every turn. In "Konzessionierte Schnüffler" [84] ("Licensed Snoopers"), Kraus states that detective bureaus are a greater menace than prostitution.

T. W. Adorno sees in Kraus's juridicial zeal the heritage of a persecuted Jew pleading his own case: he is "a Shylock who gives his heart's blood, whereas Shakespeare's Shylock wants to cut out the heart of a bourgeois."[85] On a more pragmatic level, Kraus's panopticum of legal lapses and gyrations of justice adds up to yet another powerful indictment of "Austria, the country where even the all-too-human is seen from the viewpoint of partisan stupidity." [86]

V   The Great Wall of China

Die chinesische Mauer (The Great Wall of China) was, next to *Die letzten Tage der Menschheit,* Kraus's most successful book in his lifetime, achieving five editions between 1910 and 1930. It contains material that appeared in *Die Fackel* between 1907 and 1910. In 1914, the title essay, a disquisition on the differences between Eastern and Western mentality and morality, was published separately with eight lithographs by Oskar Kokoschka. The indignation of the social satirist in *Sittlichkeit und Kriminalität,* the gloomy and bitter wit of the earlier collection now give way to lighter humor, even though the satire is just as aggressive. To use Friedrich Schiller's categorization of satire, now we get jesting satire in addition to the pathos-filled and punishing kind. The collection contains in brief compass most aspects of Kraus's later concerns, excepting, of course, the horrors of World War I and Hitlerism.

In "Prozess Veith" (October, 1908) Kraus discusses the trial of Conte Marcell Veith, who for years supervised his foster daughter, "Countess Mizzi," a prostitute. When he was suddenly arrested for procuring and sentenced to a year in prison, the girl drowned herself—officially, "because she could no longer endure that way of life."[87] Kraus begins with "Anrede an den Staat," a tirade against the state which he frequently recited in public. Veith's deeds are seen as no more reprehensible than socially accepted actions and liaisons; the morals division of the police is called "an institution created straight out of chaos,"[88] and "the existence of the lowliest *Schanddirne* [shameful prostitute] is something purer and more cultural than that of a public prosecutor. . . . What a profession that forces a man to compose indictments against nature!"[89]

In "Der Sündenpfuhl" ("The Sink of Corruption") Kraus says that "bourgeois society consists of two types of men: those who say that a den of vice has been raided somewhere and those who regret having learned the address too late."[90] Since time immemorial, indignation has fed on lust and vice versa. Sometimes the greatest perversities are committed in a seemingly moral home environment; and only among procurers is there truth. "Das Ehrenkreuz" ("The Cross of Honor") is about a prostitute who wore a military medal given her by a customer and was sentenced to a fine: "Justice is a whore that can't be skunked and collects wages of shame even from the poor."[91]

In "Der Hanswurst" ("The Clown"), Kraus states that it is better to be unjust than intellectual, that the logicality of prejudice should not be curtailed by fastening on cases in which truth has come into the world through an error. Referring to the Austrian deputy who is credited (or debited) with the statement "Culture is what one Jew copies from another" and to his own lifelong foe, the editor of the *Neue Freie Presse,* Kraus writes: "I regard Herr Bielohlawek as a more honest servant of cultural progress than Herr Benedikt." [92] Unadorned barbarism irrupts into a barbarism that is equipped with electric light and all modern conveniences; and it serves as a beneficial disturbance of an intelligence that is starving the intellect. Bielohlawek is "the clown of liberalism";[93] therefore he might well be a prophet, for the magic wand of the liberal spirit produces strange metamorphoses: its prophets are clowns and its clowns prophets.

Good examples of Kraus's lighthearted satire are "Ö.G.Z.B.D.G.," "Fahrende Sänger," "Der Biberpelz," and "Das Erdbeben." The initials in the first piece stand for "Österreichische Gesellschaft zur Bekämpfung der Geschlechtskrankheiten" [94] ("Austrian Society to Combat Venereal Disease"). This society wishes to convene a conference and invites Kraus to participate as an expert, for was he not the first to discuss syphilis in public? The conference turned out to be "öliges Geschwätz zur Beruhigung des Gewissens" ("Treacly Talk to Calm the Conscience"). But the initials could also stand for "Öde Gewohnheiten zerstören bald die Gesundheit" ("Dreary Habits Soon Destroy Health") or "Örtliche Gelegenheit zur Betätigung des Geschlechtstriebes" ("Local Opportunity to Satisfy Sexual Drive"); actually, the latter is really what the world hopes to learn about.

"Fahrende Sänger"[95] ("Traveling Minstrels"; May, 1907) is a witty piece about the world tour of the Vienna Men's Choral Society, a persiflage of banal newspaper reports on the men's eating habits and other shipboard activities on their trip to America. "Der Biberpelz" [96] is a hilarious piece about the theft of Kraus's beaver coat. This gets him more recognition than all his writings ever did. The theft in a coffee house was dignified and quiet, but the aftermath was not. The whole thing has been very painful for Kraus; he is escorted by stupidity like someone who has been robbed and is then taken prisoner. His only hope to escape this unwelcome prominence is to publish a new book; then the Viennese will forget him again.

"Stupidity is an elemental force for which no earthquake is a match"[97] is the message of "Das Erdbeben." Early in 1908 there was a minor earthquake in Vienna, and Kraus comments on the fatuous reactions it produced. It seemed to be just something for the *Neue*

Freie Presse to report and an opportunity for people to get their names in the paper; for every night table that shook a bit was duly registered. Under an assumed name, Kraus wrote a letter to the *Neue Freie Presse,* purporting to contain the observations of an engineer. Even though this letter contained palpable pseudo-scientific nonsense, it was promptly printed. The paper ignored Kraus as a satirist but prints him as a "geologist"! The whole thing seemed to Kraus like a foretaste of how the Viennese would behave when the end of the world came. This hoax, incidentally, was to have some amusing consequences. In 1911, Arthur Schütz, a Viennese wit and engineer, won a coffee-house bet by getting the *Neue Freie Presse* to print a fanciful letter supposedly from a mining engineer who reported that during an earthquake his *Gruben-hund* had shown marked signs of unrest. A *Grubenhund* is a small miner's cart attached to a crane; only a careless or ignorant reader would suppose it to be a dog. In 1916, the satirical zoo created by Kraus's circle was enlarged by the addition of the *Laufkatze,* ostensibly a kind of cat, but in reality a crane carriage or traveling trolley used in a mine. (An approximate equivalent of the gist of Schütz's letter would be a statement like "The meeowing of a cat o'nine tails keeps me awake at night.") Kraus gleefully registered the implications of such monumental put-ons, and the *Grubenhund* in particular became a widely appreciated symbol for the ignorance, presumption, and philistinism of the press, its "culturally accredited chastisement and Damoclean sword." [98] (Arthur Schütz, a master of mystification, actually plied his trade in the groves of the *Grubenhund* until recent years.)[99]

In addition to essays on Maximilian Harden, Peter Altenberg, and Alexander Girardi (on the eve of the actor's departure for Berlin, Kraus called him "a man to whom a city owes the humor of a quarter of a century"),[100] this collection contains several topical pieces. "Der Festzug" [101] ("The Parade") comments on the procession planned in 1908 in honor of Franz Joseph's sixtieth anniversay as monarch. The committee planning the celebration refused to dissolve after the Emperor had urged that the money and the labor involved go to charity instead, for the people need bread and circuses, and no one wants to be done out of a spectacle.

"Jubel und Jammer" ("Jubilation and Misery"), on the same subject, culminates in the outcry "Lord, put an end to our jubilation." [102] "Von den Sehenswürdigkeiten" deals with Vienna's sights, and Kraus believes that there are so many that the creation of new works of art becomes impossible. But, at any rate, "in our past we are way ahead of other peoples." [103] Even the service people in Vienna are sights: "The coachman has individuality, and I don't make any headway; the waiter is a thoroughbred and therefore he delays my food; the coal man sings a merry tune on his carriage while I am freezing." [104]

"Schrecken der Unsterblichkeit" ("Horrors of Immortality") is about another kind of sight. Schiller's immortality will come about only when that unfortunate immortality secured for him by mediocrities ("vermin of fame: Germanists, esthetes, reporters") [105] has vanished. The poet has to be removed from the homes where he serves as a stove decoration before he can return to them as a revolutionary. If Schiller had foreseen these types, "if he had seen them coming along, swarming about culture, reaching up to his heaven with their flat heads and trampling his earth with their flat feet so that there is no escaping the omnipotence of their love, he would have declined his immortality!" [106]

Two small contemporary nightmares are detailed in "Die Welt der Plakate" and "Die Entdeckung des Nordpols." "The World of Posters" is composed of the faces of advertisers; Kraus has bad dreams about these advertising messages which culminate in "Murder Yourself!" [107] "The Discovery of the North Pole" by Peary in 1909 seems to have brought about an inflation of all values: "The greatest man of the century" is the title of the hour; of course, someone else will hold it next year. "Progress celebrates Pyrrhic victories over nature," making "purses out of human skin!" [108] (A remark of awful prescience!). The world made more progress when people were traveling by mail coach than now when every clerk uses an airplane. "What good is speed if the brain has oozed out en route?" [109] It is stupidity which has reached the North Pole, and it has put up its flag there as a sign that it owns the world. Ice fields of the intellect cover the earth, and those who think die.

The juxtaposition of two or more newspaper items without comment, one of Kraus's most frequent and most effective techniques, may be noted in two pieces contained in this collection. In "Die weisse Kultur, oder warum in die Ferne schweifen? Aus einer Berliner Zeitung" [110] ("White Culture, or Why Roam Far? From a Berlin Newspaper"), the left-hand column carries an item from a newspaper deploring the correspondence between German girls wishing to add to their stamp collections and natives of German colonies in Africa to whom they send photos and other mementoes. The right-hand column contains a number of marriage ads from the same paper, all from men desirous of dowries or of marrying into a business. "Die Mütter"[111] ("The Mothers") presents, on the left, a chilling story about a woman who killed her illegitimate child after she had vainly appealed to the authorities and people had refused to help her, and on the right, an article on methods of baptizing an unborn child by inserting a needle with baptismal water into the mother's abdomen.

VI Heine and the Consequences: "End of the World by Black Magic"

If Kraus's one great theme was public morality, especially morality or immorality as reflected in various publications, his pursuit of this theme characteristically took the form of the peaceable satirist's unremitting warfare against the press. Journalism and the *"journaille"* (a term analogous to *"canaille"*, which Kraus popularized after it had been suggested to him by Alfred von Berger) were seen by him as the central problem, as a vast switchboard concentrating and activating the forces of corruption, decay, and dissolution. He regarded the press not merely as an economic and social menace, but as an intellectual and spiritual one as well.

Kraus recognized a disturbing identity between *Zeit* and *Zeitung,* his age and the newspapers it spawned, with *Worte* (words) usurping and destroying *Werte* (values), and news reports causing as well as describing actions. The "black magic" bringing about the end of the world was printer's ink, and Kraus had apocalyptic visions of Black Masses being celebrated in the citadels of that commodity. He once expressed the wish that everything could be printed in the *Neue Freie Presse,* for then he would be able to concentrate his fire and, Godlike, rest on the seventh day. To him the *Neue Freie Presse* stood for all Viennese journalism as the most glaring reflection of the oligarchy directing Austria's destinies by controlling the government and capital, influencing public opinion as well as the arts and sciences, and killing thought and imagination.

Because of a tradition of censorship going back to the Metternich era, Vienna's newspapers were "literary" rather than political in character. *Die Presse,* founded in 1848 by August Zang, became the *Neue Freie Presse* in 1864 under the directorship of Michael Etienne and Max Friedländer. As the organ of the Liberal party, it acquired great influence in government circles. Baron Gautsch, the sometime prime minister of Austria, once said that "without the *Neue Freie Presse* no government can stay in power in Austria."[112] Moriz Benedikt, who had joined the staff in 1872, became editor-in-chief in 1881. For a number of years he shared the direction of the paper with Eduard Bacher, but from 1908 until his death in 1920, Benedikt was in sole charge.

Kraus's embittered attacks on the *Neue Freie Presse* furnish striking evidence of his opposition to his time, for in the view of many it was the best newspaper in Austria and one of the great journals of Europe. Writing shortly before his death in 1942, Stefan Zweig described it as a pillar of the "world of yesterday":

In Vienna there was really only one journal of high grade, the *Neue Freie Presse,* which, because of its dignified principles, its cultural endeavors and its political prestige, assumed in the Austro-Hungarian monarchy a role not unlike that of the *Times* in England or the *Temps* in France. No paper, even in the German Reich, was as particular about its intellectual level. . . . As a matter of course it was progressive and liberal in its views, prudent and cautious in its politics; and it represented the high cultural aspirations of the old Austria in an exemplary fashion.[113]

Even if one allows for the likelihood that Zweig saw this newspaper through the rose-colored glasses of nostalgia for what he remembered as the "golden age of security" and for his own literary success after he had contributed to that paper's cultural section, the loneliness of Kraus's fight becomes apparent. Kraus's opposition to this paper in particular may be viewed as his special form of revolt against a father image, just as his *Hassliebe* for the Austrian-Jewish spirit may be regarded as a deep-rooted father complex. Kraus was convinced that the moving forces of his time were not entrenched in parliaments but in newspaper offices and that the state had long ago abdicated the real power of leadership to anonymous, irresponsible, and reprehensible powers. He was in agreement with the insight expressed by Kierkegaard fifty years earlier that if Christ were born now, his target would not be high priests but journalists.[114]

Decades before Hermann Hesse coined the phrase *"feuilleton-istisches Zeitalter"* in his novel *Magister Ludi,*[115] Karl Kraus recognized his time as a feuilletonistic age in which newspaper reports were more important than events, the form towered over the content and in which the style, the atmosphere, the "package" were all-important. In attempting to get at the roots of this situation, Kraus had to come to terms with an important component of his own German-Jewish heritage. In 1910 he wrote a pamphlet entitled *Heine und die Folgen (Heine and the Consequences)*, reprinting it in *Die Fackel* the following year because the publication had not been widely noticed. (Seven years later, the pamphlet was in its third printing and later it was included in the collection *Untergang der Welt durch schwarze Magie.*) Already in 1906 Kraus had written an essay "Um Heine", which was still a rather positive assessment of the German-Jewish poet and satirist.[116] It is clear why Kraus had to deal with Heine, for Heine, too, had overcome journalism and graduated to the world of literature; and he, too, stood, as it were, between Jehovah and Wotan. Heine seems to have given Kraus his cues for a sustained tirade against the journalistic mind.

As Kraus saw him, Heine provided a great inheritance on which journalism has drawn to this day: its function as a dangerous intermediary between art and life and as a parasite on both The instrument has degenerated into an ornament, and Heine ornamented German concerns with French *esprit*. As Kraus puts it, "Without Heine no feuilleton." [117] This is the French disease with which he has infected us. "Heine ... has so loosened the corsets of the German language that today every little merchant can fondle her breasts." [118] He has made talents indistinguishable; everything is made to resemble, and go with, everything else; and this has led to a confusion of linguistic values. Everything is talked to death. If there is a streetcar accident in Vienna, they write atmospherically about the nature of streetcars, the nature of streetcar accidents, the nature of accidents in general, all viewed from the perspective "What is man?" Kraus objects to the blending of intellectual with informational elements, to journalists brazenly encroaching upon literature. "Collections of feuilletons appear, and the most astonishing thing about them is that they didn't crumble in the hands of the bookbinders."[119]

Kraus also points to basic differences between the German and French languages. French surrenders more easily, lends itself more readily to the blandishments of the feuilleton form and promotes laziness of thought, mere dalliance, and a superficial brilliance. "If one says of a German writer that he must have been trained by the French, it is the highest praise only if it is not true" [120], for this means that he owes to the German language what the French language gives to everyone. Ever since Heine imported the trick, it has hardly been necessary for a feuilletonist to go to Paris in order to develop his talent: "Today they credit a lame man who stays in Vienna with the ability to do the can-can." [121] Those who do go to Paris, however, "throw the quicksand of the French language, which blows into the hands of every fool, into the eyes of the German reader." [122]

Heine has thus created a facile pattern, blending substance with form; and this linguistically deceitful pattern has since become the journalistic norm. "To write a feuilleton is to curl locks on a bald pate—but the public likes these curls better than a lion's mane of thought." [123] Heine irresponsibly opened the floodgates to this deleterious development, making talents out of nontalents. Life is now swamped with ornaments, the literary as well as the architectural kind. [124] False literary material is introduced into journalism, and emptiness and corruption are given a high gloss. Journalists choose great, "eternal" themes, but their writings become obsolete as soon as they are reprinted. Every Heine epigone has taken a stone from his mosaic, and now none is left.

While paying due respects to the late, genuine poetry of Heine, Kraus believes that "Heine the poet lives only as a youthful love that has been preserved" [125] but is badly in need of revision, for in this case literary judgments are beclouded by the syrup of sentimentality. But Kraus also lampoons people who hate Heine, the Jew, and then intone "Die Lorelei." Heine's verses are operetta lyrics; in his poetry ideas are not crystallized but candied; and his verses are nothing but "scanned journalism" [126] which keeps the reader abreast of Heine's moods. As a result, neither lyricism nor satire is really present. Kraus calls Heine's wit, in prose as well as poetry, "an asthmatic cur." [127] Devoid of substance, it does not keep its promises; it is merely "the summer lightning of ideas which have struck or will strike somewhere." [128] Heine's cynicism, that "stale pie of wit and woe," [129] is very much to the Germans' taste, and "journalistic piety demands that in every newspaper office there be at least one bedbug from Heine's mattress grave" [130] to crawl through the columns of the Sunday paper.

"Only in the rapture of linguistic creation does the chaos become world" [131], writes Kraus, and his basic quarrel with Heine is that he, "a linguistic daredevil . . . never lowered his eyes before language." [132] Language did his bidding, but it never vouchsafed him silent ecstasy; its grace never forced him to his knees. "He was a Moses who beat the rock of the German language with his rod. But speed is not magic. The water did not flow from the rock, but he had brought it along in his other hand; and it was *eau de Cologne.*" [133]

The collection *Untergang der Welt durch schwarze Magie (End of the World by Black Magic)* (1922) contains material that appeared in the

Fackel between 1908 and 1912. In the title essay, based on newspaper clippings, Kraus lashes out at "feuilletonism" by saying that newspapers ruin all thought by prepackaging facts together with imagination, preventing the reader from using his own mind and rendering him unreceptive to art because its superficial values have been skimmed off. He excoriates the meretricious and mendacious journalistic poaching on the preserves of poets and foretells the doom of a society which commits and tolerates incursions into cultural areas and values for the adornment of daily life. The effect is that "nowhere on earth can one experience the end as vividly as in Austria." [134]

"Apokalypse," written in October, 1908, predicts the end of the *Fackel* because of the "feverish progress of human stupidity." [135] "What can a writer of satire do in the face of goings-on which are answered every hour by the mocking laughter of hell? . . . The real end of the world is the destruction of the spirit; the other kind depends on the insignificant attempt to see whether after such a destruction the world can go on." [136] In the same piece, Kraus bemoans the Sunday editions of newspapers which now take the place of trees; for one edition of a paper requires pulp derived from ten thousand trees, and it is easier to reprint than to reforest. Kraus's poem "The Newspaper" expands on this theme:

> Do you, who read the paper, know
> How many forest-trees lie bleeding,
> so that you, blinded by such reading,
> may in this mirror see yourself and go
> about your money-mucking and your feeding?

> Do you, who read the paper, know
> how many men are daily dying,
> so that a few may, by its prying,
> enjoy the profits of the gruesome show,
> and others yet its gossip and its lying?

> And can you, knowing this, still read the paper?
> Must not this newsprint blind an eye that sees?
> How the fraud grew from nothing by degrees
> and to a substance threatening, this vapor!
> I cannot see the wood for blighted trees! [137]

In "Philosophen" Kraus muses on what could be done with journalists if there were no newspapers. They might become philosophers; but philosophers who write for journals are superfluous. As for historians, they are "people who don't write well enough to work on a daily paper. . . . Literary history is lack of talent for journalism." [138] Kraus has the Midas touch in "that every passage in a newspaper, a periodical, a publisher's prospectus that my finger touches has turned into tin." [139] Given his special gift for absorbing, fixing, and standardizing all impressions of public life, he calls for an eight days' moratorium on the meanness, the "progress," and the social life of the world, so that the stockpile of old events can be reduced. "Because the invention of the art of printing, not the comet, is causing the end of the world, the desired intermission ought at least to be brought about by a typesetters' strike." [140] Again and again Kraus castigates the deleterious mixture of intellect and information, reportage and literature, *Tachles* (brass tacks) with *Schmonzes* (trivia), fact with fancy.

Before the war Austria-Hungary experienced many of the cultural conflicts and much of the social and spiritual deterioration which the rest of Europe faced after 1918. Amidst the hedonistic pursuits of "gay Vienna" there lurked the despair which Kierkegaard refers to as the "sickness unto death." The decay of the old Austrian civilization was accompanied by a spiritual crisis which manifested itself most palpably in a crisis of communication—the very disintegration of language. This is the aspect of the *fin de siècle* and the early years of the new century which seemed predestined for Kraus's satire, and he regarded the press as "the goiter of the world" [141], as the polluter of language, and as the poisoner of the human spirit. The vehemence of his attacks may have stemmed, in part, from his realization that the vaunted Austrian *Gemütlichkeit* and disarming inefficiency might have absorbed a milder satirist and accepted him as just another literary entertainer and culture clown. In the dying decades of the old Austria, Kraus truly was an "apocalyptic humorist." "No one else so mocked, vilified, crushingly attacked Austria during his entire life," writes Hans Weigel, "because no one loved Vienna and Austria more and suffered more because of it." [142]

CHAPTER 4

The Prostitute Turned into a Virgin: Kraus and Language

I *Language and Morality*

With hungry heart and burning brain
night after night I sought her.
As a brazen whore I caught her,
and made her a virgin again.[1]

The above epigram and the related aphorism "My language is the common prostitute that I turn into a virgin" [2] illuminate both Kraus's mission and his method; yet the quest expressed in such statements does not seem to differ significantly from what many poets have striven to do: to restore pristine purity to language and make it once more a vehicle for poetic expression. Kraus's obsession with language, however, went considerably beyond such a pursuit. As Heinrich Fischer has pointed out, Kraus was "one of the most marked egocentrics of art, filled with a metaphysical compulsion to trace in himself the divine and intellectual center of language and represent it through himself." [3]

Kraus's view of language is indebted to some ideas of the German Romanticists. Novalis believed in the traditional oneness of poet and priest; his view of language as Delphi, as the dynamic element of the spiritual realm, points to the oracular quality of language and to self-knowledge. In his view, a phenomenon can be plumbed through language by being broken down into its components and their interrelationships. And Friedrich Schlegel believed that there is a poetry whose salient point is the relationship between the real and the ideal; it begins as satire with the absolute divergence between the ideal and the real, then hovers in the middle as elegy, and ends as idyl with the absolute identity of both. This view would encompass Kraus's own transition from satire to elegy and idyl.

While Kraus shared with the Romanticists an appreciation of Shakespeare as a supreme verbal artist, he went beyond the historical, philosophical, and critical writings of these poets and theorists and strove to give artistic form to such insights about language. While the greatest poetic users of language, such as Goethe, Lichtenberg, Jean Paul, and Nietzsche, were his respected models and counselors, Kraus set himself up as the ultimate judge of language, trusting his *Sprachgefühl,* his language-consciousness and linguistic instincts, implicitly, and feeling that he could never go astray while groping his way along the rope of language. He wanted to be judged by timelessness as the highest tribunal, with language as the chief witness. "His Jehovah is language, and he is its high priest." [4]

"Word and essence [*Wort und Wesen*] —that is the only connection I have ever striven for in my life," [5] Kraus wrote. He saw an absolute congruity between word and thought, language and life. Since he believed in a correspondence between language and experience, the unworthiness of his age was for him defined by its treatment of language. "In me language itself, the bearer of the most revolting life-substance, rebels against this substance," Kraus wrote in *Pro domo et mundo.* "It spontaneously mocks, screams, and shakes with disgust. Life and language come to blows with each other until they burst, and the end is an unarticulated jumble—the true style of our time." [6]

One of Kraus's most characteristic poems, "Bekenntnis" ("Confession"), contains at once his self-portrait and his program:

> Ich bin nur einer von den Epigonen
> die in dem alten Haus der Sprache wohnen. . . .[7]

Kraus is one of the *epigoni* who dwell in the old house of language and are able to estimate the worth of their ancestors, the great masters of language. Yet he claims primacy for his own experiences in that house; he breaks out and destroys Thebes. Even though he was late-born, he reserves the right to take bloody revenge in behalf of his fathers, to avenge language on all those who speak and abuse it in his time, on the *"kundige Thebaner"* [learned Thebans] who think that they master their language and their age and yet must succumb to the individual who sets out to sack Thebes. Kraus identified defective use of language with a defective moral and metaphysical outlook; for him linguistic obtuseness was invariably equated with intellectual or ethical obtuseness. In *Nachts,* he wrote: "This is something I cannot get over—that a whole line could be written by half a man. That a work could be built on the quicksand of a character." [8]

Georg Christoph Lichtenberg, the eighteenth-century physicist, aphorist, and satirist, foreshadowed Kraus's attitude when he wrote: "I have often wished that there might be a language in which it would be impossible ever to say a falsehood, or where at least every lapse from the truth would be a lapse from grammar." [9] Kraus felt that German was, or could be, such a language, and when he refers to *"die Sprache,"* the *German* language is meant. "What a way of life would develop if Germans took their orders from no other authority than that of language!" he wrote in the title essay of *Die Sprache*.[10] In connection with Kraus, Leopold Liegler speaks of *"Sprachmystik"* and defines "language mysticism" as "the unfathomable experience ... that in the chosen word idea, form, color and mood come about in such a mysterious way that the outer world is not only designated but, by virtue of the associative potential supplied by the word, interpreted as well." [11] Elsewhere Liegler writes that "one can compare Karl Kraus's relationship to language with the animistic attitude of those primitive religions which believe in linguistic magic and hope to effect something in the outer world by pronouncing a word." [12] Kraus's view of language thus is not a rationalistic one, for the very first version of a word is derived from an artistic experience based on belief in a prestabilized harmony of word and world. To Kraus language is not just a means of communication but a method of uncovering intellectual and spiritual connections.

Kraus always emphasized the connection between language and morality; for him language was the moral criterion for a writer or speaker. Yet J. P. Stern sees fallacies and pitfalls in what he calls Kraus's "moral-linguistic imperative": "We cannot, on the social scene, identify linguistic insensitivity and obtuseness and even downright abuse of language with moral torpor or degeneracy—though we may see in them signs of ignorance, or of a poor education, or thoughtlessness in verbal matters. . . . On the other hand, the use of language as an indicator of positive values is, if anything, even more problematic; there is at least one occasion when Kraus's insistence on the sublime literary value of a political manifesto landed him in an attitude one would like to call absurd were it not irresponsible." [13] The reference is to Kraus's evaluation of Emperor Franz Joseph's manifesto *"An meine Völker"* of August, 1914 as an "exalted ... most humane proclamation ... a poem" *("erhabenster ... menschlichster Anschlag ... Gedicht").*[14] Stern expresses a basic objection to Kraus's absolute equation between word and world when he writes: "To say that the imagination, or the sensibility, of a man is coextensive with his morality is very much like saying that his language is coextensive with his experience. These two assertions encompass Kraus's entire work, and both are open to the same logical and existential objections. One finally wonders whether, in basing his entire work on these two equations, Kraus was not, after all, succumbing to the curse of Vienna—the city in which the experiment of replacing morality and politics by the life of the imagination was carried to the point of moral paralysis and political disintegration." [15] There is some evidence that Kraus tried to break out of this self-imposed limit, e.g., his aphorism "Language is the only chimera whose illusory power is endless, the inexhaustibility which keeps life from being impoverished. Let men learn to serve language!" [16]

In a series of striking aphorisms, Kraus stressed the connection between thought and language and his belief that in its subliminal existence the word triggers the linguistically preformed idea which brings the word into being: "Language is the mother of thought, not its handmaiden";[17] "Language is the mother of thought? A thought is not to the credit of the thinker? Oh, but it is; the thinker has to impregnate language";[18] "Let language be the divining rod that finds sources of thought";[19] "I have derived many a thought that I do not have and could not express in words from language";[20] "Because I take an idea *beim Wort* [by the word *or* at its word] , it comes." [21]

Dichtung, creative writing, meant to Kraus exclusively *Sprachgestaltung,* linguistic form. That is why he regarded Johann Nestroy as a greater dramatist than Franz Grillparzer and preferred the obscurest bit of local news, or its literary representation by a Peter Altenberg, to a novel—because in that form the subject, the substance, is more important than the sentence, which is the sole carrier of verbal art. Linguistic creativeness and conciseness, he felt, are not so important in a novel as narrative skill and the psychological penetration of the characters. "Opinions, trends, *Weltanschauungen*—," he wrote in 1921, "what matters first and last is only the sentence. . . . There probably has never been a writer from whom more substantial, more real, more timely things could be derived than the author of my writings; and yet all my life I have cared about nothing but sentences, trusting that the truth about mankind, its wars and revolutions, its Jews and Christians, will occur to them." [22]

The German word *Satz* has the dual meaning of "sentence" (or "proposition") and "leap" (in English, "sentence" in the double sense of a grammatical unit and a judgment would be an equivalent example); and when Kraus pronounced it, he sometimes made a slight motion indicating a jump. "My mission is a profane one and my realm is entirely of this linguistic world," [23] he wrote. Kraus had a passionate conviction that the flood of words in the daily press was not only corrupting language but life itself. Undertaking to dam (and damn) this flood himself, he caught even the smallest and least limpid waves and used them to demonstrate that the flood was indeed a pernicious one. "In no language is there such bad speech and writing as in the German language, and in no German-speaking region are things as bad as in Austria. Vienna is suffering the fate of Babel insofar as the Lord has there confused one single people's speech." [24] Throughout, he pointed to the great tradition of the German language ("The German language is the deepest, German speech the shallowest")[25] and attempted to resuscitate its long-buried values and beauties.

Despite the fact that Kraus raised language to an almost apocalyptic significance, he never developed a philosophy of language, being essentially an antiphilosophical thinker; and his aphorisms and essays do not add up to any systematic theory of language. Kraus had a sort of philosophical gap, one through which language was able to enter. What differentiated him from academic philologists was his lack of interest in the history of language and in etymology; he cared only about the pragmatic and creative aspects of language, past and present. The "Vienna Circle" of logical positivists found Kraus's relationship to language to be of interest, and there are certain parallels between Kraus's thought and the ideas of Ludwig Wittgenstein, the foremost thinker of logical positivism. The philosopher believed that ethics and esthetics are one, and Paul Engelmann has pointed out that "the insight into the fundamental connection between esthetics and ethics is also a basic element in Kraus's critique of poetic language." [26]

Like Kraus, Wittgenstein believed in an inextricable connection between all forms of living, thinking, feeling, and the forms of language. In 1915 he wrote: "The limits of my language stand for the limits of my world." [27] In his main work, the *Tractatus Logico-Philosophicus* of 1921, he comes to the conclusion that all philosophy is a critique of language; and his work may be read as an effort to guard against the bewitching of our intellect by language, to distinguish the sayable from that which cannot be said, to limit the scope of what can be represented through words, and to protect the unutterable by uttering it. Wittgenstein learned from Kraus how to think in and through language, yet he thought *against* language—which, for him was an obstacle to thought that had to be painstakingly surmounted—

whereas Kraus fought *for* language, mystically discovering thought through it.

Wittgenstein's concept of "mystical silence" is akin to Kraus's wartime invitation to those who really had something to say in the cacophony of "patriotic" verbiage to step forward and—be silent. The logical positivists' view of the corruption of language as an inevitable development may be contrasted with Kraus's attempt to rescue language from its function as an instrument of cultural decadence. "In appraising the intellectual link which exists between Karl Kraus and Wittgenstein," writes J. P. Stern, "it would . . . be necessary to consider 1) the background common to them both—Vienna in the first quarter of this century, 2) their experience of it as a linguistic (because moral) Babel; and 3) their determination to build, each from his own vision of language, a fortress that should stand inviolate against the corruption of words and morals around them."[28]

II *Pathos and Puns*

It is all but impossible to convey in English an idea of Karl Kraus's style, the most brilliant in modern German literature, a style that attempted to make a diagnosis of the linguistic and moral sickness of what Kraus regarded as a language-forsaken age. The allusiveness of this style, its attention to associations among words, and its artful plays upon words make the reading of Kraus's works an intellectual delight of a high order; yet very little of this stylistic brilliance can be transferred to another language. Kraus regarded it as desirable that his writings be read at least twice, for while the contents might be absorbed at a first reading, the stylistic artistry would become apparent only after closer attention. He said that a sentence should not be there for people to rinse their mouths with and contrasted his art with the writers of feuilletons who attract at the first glance and disappoint at the second.

Kraus was not only a master of the art of punning, with a deep seriousness underlying his verbal wit, but a skillful practitioner of amphibology, the ambiguity of speech that stems from the uncertainty of grammatical construction rather than the meaning of words, with a phrase or sentence capable of being construed in more than one way. Because of its great intensity and economy of verbal means, Kraus's prose invites close attention. One finite verb can resolve several phrases; the links between nouns and pronouns are not always readily apparent, conjunctions are often dispensed with; and the style is generally elliptical. A good example of the tension in Kraus's prose—a quality which, unfortunately, is largely dissipated in translation—is this passage from the speech *"In dieser grossen Zeit. . . ."* which Kraus made on November 19, 1914:

In these great times which I knew when they were this small; which will become small again, provided they have time left for it; and which—because in the realm of organic growth no such transformation is possible—we had better call fat times and, truly, hard times as well; in these times in which things are happening that could not be imagined and in which that which one can no longer *imagine* must *happen,* for if one could imagine it, it would not happen; in these serious times which have died laughing at the thought that they might become serious; which, surprised by their own tragedy, are reaching for diversion and, catching themselves redhanded, are groping for words; in these loud times which boom with the horrible symphony of deeds that produce reports and reports that cause deeds; in these times you should not expect any words of my own from me—none but these words which barely manage to prevent silence from being misinterpreted. Respect for the immutability, the subordination of language before this misfortune is too deeply rooted in me.[29]

At the center of this dialectically constructed periodic sentence Kraus places an "inspiring" platitude mouthed by every orator, militarist, and teacher in wartime: we live in "great times." Deflating this cliché by depriving it of its aura, he dismembers and varies the title of his speech while he withholds the main clause. His central assertion is the great rift between thought and action, events and the imagination, the sword and the pen, language and experience, the press and truth. After usurping from the outward world one of its hateful phrases, he "places it before the court of his linguistic conscience and imagination; cross-examines the phrase by means of various antithetic devices, exploring a wealth of denotations, of literal, metaphorical and idiomatic meanings, and the record of the cross-examination turns out to be the portrait of an age."[30]

In his poem "Abenteuer der Arbeit" ("Adventures of Work"), Kraus places plays upon words at the center of his thought: . . . "Im Wortspiel sind enthalten Gedanken, die mich finden . . ."[31] ("A play upon words contains thoughts that reach me . . ."). "A pun, though despicable in itself," he wrote elsewhere, "can be the noblest vehicle of an artistic intention by serving as the abbreviation of a witty view. It can be social criticism in the form of an epigram."[32] Punning often constitutes a *reductio ad absurdum* of language and serves as a divining rod for the truthfulness or untruthfulness of a statement or a mentality.[33] Only in rare instances can an exact equivalent for this verbal play be found. "It is a chlorious war" for "Es ist ein chlorreicher Krieg"[34] is a case in point. The sardonic insight that in some circles *Monogamie* (monogamy) was literally translated as, or equated with, *Einheirat* (marrying into a business) was one of many that Kraus owed to his language. In his puns the key is often supplied by some visual feature, as for example, in "A man can't be unappetizing enough for me not to *angreifen* him"[35] (*"Angreifen"* can mean "touch" or "attack"); or in "Every artistic presentation should bear this warning: The public is requested only to look at the objects displayed, not to grasp [*begreifen*] them."[36] A statement like "Je grösser der Stiefel, desto grösser der Absatz"[37] plays on the multiple meanings of *Stiefel* (boot; nonsense) and *Absatz* (heel; paragraph; sale). Even a translation like "The greater the bull, the bigger the bull-market" cannot convey all the levels of meaning in Kraus's aphorism.

III *Aphorisms and Words in Verse*

Kraus was not only a prose writer *par excellence,* but also a poet. The aphorism is a prose form which occupies an important place in his work. Aphoristic thoughts are apt to appear in Kraus's writings in various guises: Some aphorisms were distilled from a longer text in prose or poetry; in other cases they were lyrically expanded into an epigram or served as the nucleus of a prose piece.[38] Three volumes of aphorisms, drawn from the *Fackel,* appeared in Kraus's lifetime: *Sprüche und Widersprüche* (*Dicta and Contradictions,* 1909); *Pro domo et mundo* (1912); and *Nachts* (*At Night,* 1918). Some of Kraus's aphoristic statements about that literary form are in themselves notable and revealing: "One cannot dictate an aphorism to a typist. It would take too long."[39] (This could be taken to mean that even the fastest typist could not handle the flash of inspiration, or that the cerebral process producing an aphorism is endless and that no typist could wait long enough.) "Someone who can write aphorisms should not fritter his time away in essays."[40] "An aphorism need not be true, but it should overtake truth. It must get beyond it *in einem Satz*" ("in one sentence" or "with one leap").[41] "An aphorism never coincides with truth; it is either a half-truth or a truth-and-a-half."[42]

Kraus began to write poetry comparatively late in life; his first poems appeared in the *Fackel* in 1912 and 1913. Nine volumes of poetry under the title *Worte in Versen (Words in Verse)* were published between 1916 and 1930. In his verse Kraus admittedly is an epigone rather than an innovator; the poet is indebted to Goethe and Shakespeare. He was "unoriginal" in that he needed some occasion to trigger his art, the way an oyster needs the irritation of a grain of sand to produce a pearl. His poems are seldom "romantic" in the sense that they are products of poetic rapture or intoxication; rather, they spring from the rapture of language and logic.

Kraus made little distinction between lyrical or pathetic prose satire and the poetic language of his verse. Some of his poems are versified glosses and polemics, autobiographic excursions, lyrical versions of *Fackel* texts, or satiric ideas given purified form. Their abstractness and concision often presuppose familiarity with Kraus's other works, his life, and his personality. "I do not write poetry and then work with dross," Kraus wrote; "I turn the dross into poems and then organize rallies in support of poetry." [43] Elsewhere he wrote: "Satire is the poetry of the obstacle, richly compensated for being the obstacle of poetry." [44] To a certain extent Kraus's poetry is *Gedankenlyrik* in Schiller's sense—poetry with a cargo of thought, reflecting a tradition coming to an end. Yet it also represents a sort of satirist's holiday in the sense that Kraus is here free to reveal himself fully and unabashedly in his love of mankind, the human spirit, nature, and animals. Poetry, to him, was like a freer, purer world, one harking back to the German classical tradition, in which the poet, freed from the goads of the satiric occasion and an ever wakeful moral conscience, was able to reflect on love, nature, fear, and wonderment.

In his poetry Kraus was guided by his conviction that the quality of a poem depended on the moral quality of the poet. ("A poem is good until one knows by whom it is.")[45] In his view, a satirist was only a deeply hurt lyricist, the artist wounded by the ugliness of the world. In the *Worte in Versen,* rhyme and meaning are inseparably fused. Kraus's idea of rhyme is similar to that of Friedrich Schlegel, who had described it as the surprising reunion of friendly ideas after a long separation. If one gives it aphoristic (and macaronic) form, Kraus's definition reads "Rhyme is the landing shore/ for two thoughts *en rapport.*" In the context of his poem "Der Reim," "It is the shore fixed for their landing,/ When two thoughts reach an understanding . . ."[46]

Kraus's poetry was never fully appreciated in his lifetime; it was decried as too unoriginal, intellectual, and not elemental enough. Yet when one realizes that much of Kraus's prose is lyrical, it is easy to see the poetry as only a special coinage from the same mint.

In his orphic epigram "Zwei Läufer,"[47] written in 1910, Kraus describes two runners sprinting along the track of time; one is bold; the other, worried. The one coming from "nowhere" reaches his goal; the one from the "origin" falls by the wayside. Yet the runner who has reached his goal makes way for his worried competitor who, however, always reaches the origin. Kraus here depicts two antithetical forces alive in the human spirit—one that he loves and one that he hates. The world is seen as a circuitous route back to the source; intellectuality may be the wrong road, yet it does lead back to immediacy; satire is a roundabout way to poetry, and poetry, to Kraus, is a philological or linguistic detour on the way to a lost paradise.

Karl Kraus placed himself midway between *Ursprung* and *Untergang,* the origin or source of all things and the end of the world as conjured up by his satiric vision; and he saw language as the only means of going back to the origin—the origin that was forever the goal. Kraus was well aware of the difficulties as well as the rewards of his mission. "The closer the look one takes at a word, the greater the distance from which it looks back,"[48] he wrote, expressing the profundity and endlessness of his preoccupation with language and his desire to plumb fathomless depths. Both the triumph and the tragedy of his lonely linguistic quest are summed up in his insight that "only he is an artist who can make a riddle out of a solution."[49]

CHAPTER 5

"The Last Days of Mankind"

> And let me speak to the yet unknowing world
> How these things came about: so shall you hear
> Of carnal, bloody, and unnatural acts;
> Of accidental judgments, casual slaughters;
> Of deaths put on by cunning and forced cause;
> And, in this upshot, purposes mistook
> Fall'n on the inventors' heads: all this can I
> Truly deliver.
>
> —*Hamlet* (Act V, Sc. 2, l. 378 ff.)

I   *The Trumpets of the Day*

If prewar Austria had seemed like an "experiment station for world destruction" to Kraus, the outbreak of World War I forced him to bear witness to what he regarded as such a destruction. The war not only confirmed the satirist's dire predictions but caused his vision of doom to assume apocalyptic dimensions. The period from 1914 to 1918 marks a decisive caesura in Kraus's life and creativity; like a vast funnel, the war and what was happening to the human spirit in wartime caught and intensified Kraus's satire, leading the satirist not only to vary, refine, and deepen the multifarious themes of his prewar writings but to set himself up as the lonely, bold, and inexorable chronicler of "the last days of mankind" for the benefit of a posterity that might no longer inhabit this planet.

Walter Benjamin has pointed out that all of Kraus's writings are "an inverted silence," [1] with the storm of events rushing into the black cloak of this silence and turning its loud lining inside out. Kraus's first reaction to the new "great times" was silence. The torch was temporarily estinguished, and for some months the torch-bearer was too stunned to participate in the flood of words around him. Kraus refused to join the majority of his literary contemporaries in jumping on the bandwagon of banality and rushing to the ramparts of rhyme. The fact that his physical condition precluded military service was reason enough for him to fear that any early reaction on his part would be widely misinterpreted. Yet he felt constrained to speak out. "Since a voiceless sacrifice . . . has still less value and effectiveness than a word, since it is not even as exemplary an act as a murder, or as many things that everyone can, may, and must do today—for this very reason the word has automatically become free." [2] "In dieser grossen Zeit . . . ," the speech he made in November, 1914, and published in the *Fackel* the following month, is the germ cell of his extensive wartime output. Kraus believed that "an ear which hears the trumpets of the Last Judgment is certainly not closed to the trumpets of the day." [3] It was, in fact, in the cacophonous blaring of the latter that Kraus heard the former. Considering the keen acoustic sense which informs his writings, it follows that Kraus's wartime work is, as it were, an enormous phonomontage based on these trumpets; they gave rise to it and are preserved in it.

II Die letzten Tage der Menschheit

The very titles of Kraus's wartime writings in book form underline the apocalyptic nature of his vision: *Nachts (At Night),* a book of aphorisms issued in 1918; *Weltgericht (Day of Judgment),* two volumes of essays published in 1919; and *Die letzten Tage der Menschheit (The Last Days of Mankind),* a mammoth drama published as a book of almost eight hundred pages in 1922. To adapt Clausewitz's phrase, Kraus's monumental play represents a continuation of his satiric writings by other means. Man's stupidity and cupidity, human suffering and degradation had reached such a fever pitch in wartime that Kraus's prewar criticism was superseded by the more urgent task of shouldering the enormous moral burden of mankind and giving it artistic expression, turning a vast amount of unpromising raw material into a work of art and once again putting his age between quotation marks.[4]

Kraus's chief target was the discrepancy between semblance and truth, the wholesale abandonment of the spirit, morality, and true humanity during the years of carnage. He felt that "what is at stake in the war is the life or death of language." [5] Characteristically, he did not wait for the detachment which might have been afforded him after the end of the war; most of the 209 scenes of his five acts were first sketched during the summers of 1915, 1916, and 1917; the Prologue dates from July, 1915, the Epilogue from July, 1917. Parts of the play were published in several special issues of *Die Fackel* and in *Worte in Versen* and read by Kraus in numerous wartime recitals; the final revisions, however, were not made until after the war. In Kraus's lifetime, only the Epilogue, "Die letzte Nacht" ("The Last Night"), was performed on the stage,[6] the satirist having refused offers by Max Reinhardt and Erwin Piscator to stage this essentially unperformable play. Kraus made a "stage version" of the drama and read it publicly in Vienna and elsewhere in 1930. In recent years an abridged version of the work—prepared by Heinrich Fischer and Leopold Lindtberg—has been seen on stage and television.[7]

In his Preface, Kraus wrote:

The performance of this drama, which would, in earthly terms, require about ten evenings, is intended for a theater on Mars. Theatergoers of this world would not be able to bear it. For it is blood of their blood, and its contents are those unreal, unthinkable years, out of reach for the wakefulness of the mind, inaccessible to any memory and preserved only in gory dreams, when characters from an operetta enacted the tragedy of mankind. . . . The humor is only the self-reproach of a man who was not driven insane by the thought that he survived being a witness to these actualities with his mind intact. . . . The most improbable deeds which are here reported really happened; I have depicted only what men did. The most improbable conversations which are here conducted were spoken word for word; the most glaring inventions are quotations. . . . Documents have a living shape; reports come to life as persons, persons die as editorials; feuilletons have been given mouths to deliver themselves as monologues; clichés stand on two legs—men have kept only one. Inflections of voices rush and rattle through the times and swell to the chorus of the unholy plot. People who have lived amidst mankind and have survived it—the executive organs and spokesmen of an age that has no flesh but blood, no blood but ink—are reduced to shadows and puppets in keeping with their busy sham existences. Ghouls and lemures, masks of the tragic carnival, have living names because this must be so and because nothing is accidental in this age conditioned by chance. This gives no one the right to regard it as a local affair. Even what happens on the corner of Kärntnerstrasse and Ringstrasse in Vienna is directed from a cosmic point. Let anyone who has weak nerves—though they may be strong enough to tolerate the times—remove himself from this play. Our contemporaries cannot be expected to regard this horror which has assumed verbal form as anything but a joke, particularly when it resounds from the cozy depths of the most horrible dialects, nor can they be expected to view what they have just lived through and survived as anything but an objectionable fiction. . . . There may also be reason to fear that a future sprung from the loins of such an unspeakable present will, despite its greater detachment, lack the greater power of comprehension.[8]

Kraus closes with Horatio's lines from the closing scene of *Hamlet* which head this chapter.

Die letzten Tage der Menschheit, originally subtitled "Ein Angst-traum" ("A Nightmare"), begins with the voice of a newspaper vendor and ends with the voice of God. This "most uncanny work that was written during the four-year mass murder" [9] spans the period from June, 1914, to the end of the war. It is set in public rather than private places—in the streets of Vienna and Berlin, in offices and barracks, churches and coffee houses, amusement places and military hospitals, railroad stations and army posts, "in a hundred scenes and hells." [10] The play's approximately five hundred characters include pastors and prostitutes, professors and politicians, teachers and tradesmen, soldiers and sycophants, children and churchmen, journalists and jesters, emperors and editors. There are actual persons and fictitious ones whose authentic speech patterns reveal and often judge them. Some apparitions are mute, but their silence speaks volumes. "What in the final analysis," asks Max Spalter, "is *The Last Days of Mankind* but a series of character analyses on the basis of the spoken word? . . . Whether the language is bureaucratically dense or resonates with the peculiar accents and intonations of colloquial usage, Kraus carries through brilliantly his aim to make language the moral index of a dying way of life. A world literally talks its way to perdition." [11]

The play is a striking amalgam of naturalistic and symbolic elements. The scenes are, by turns, lyrical and prosaic, comic and tragic; but even what seems to be purely humorous acquires a certain grimness from the context and usually appears as gallows humor. The play has no hero or plot in the conventional Aristotelian sense; it is episodic, with scenes recurring in cyclical patterns and inexorably grinding on to a cataclysmic conclusion. The scenes range in length from one-line "black-outs" in the tradition of the cabaret (more often than not, what is "blacked out" is the human spirit) to lengthy dialogues, dramatized editorials, and phantasmagoric tableaux. At first glance these seem accidental, aleatory, repetitious, or even contradictory; but the recurrence of certain motifs soon allows the reader to see larger connections. As with most of Kraus's glosses, the material in this play is eminently scenic; the speech, the intonation, and the gestures of those who appear are, as it were, caught in an acoustic mirror. "We know no other work in world literature," writes Franz Mautner, "which utilizes so many different modes of speech for mimetic or satiric characterization."[12]

The ten scenes of the Prologue range from June 28, 1914, the day on which the successor to the Austrian throne, Archduke Franz Ferdinand, and his wife were assassinated, to their third-class funeral; these scenes mercilessly lay bare the attitudes of Austrian society. A thin veneer of *Gemütlichkeit*, easygoing geniality, masks a streak of brutality and an unprincipled adherence to pseudo-values. As at the beginning of every act, hawkers and gawkers set the tone; the mindless banter of pencil-pushing playboy officers belies the newspaper reporters' attempts to depict a concerned populace. "Venedig in Wien," the Viennese Venice in the Prater amusement park, is doing business as usual, and people continue to indulge in their trivial pursuits, having stylized themselves in a veritable cult of Vienna and Viennese attitudes. The last word belongs to a newspaper editor concerned with capturing the *"Stimmung"* or atmosphere of the funeral party; he reminds a reporter to describe how the mourners prayed.[13]

Act One (along with each succeeding act) opens at the Sirk-Ecke, a then-fashionable meeting place and promenade across the street from the Opera. A few weeks after the beginning of the war, "patriotic" slogans have already caught on, stultifying and dehumanizing those who use them with bourgeois bravado or proletarian pathos. A park-bench orator speaks of a *"heiliger Verteilungskrieg"* instead of a *"Verteidigungskrieg,"* a holy war of distribution rather than one of self-defense. The crowd echoes and mouths catchwords like the brutally rhymed "Serbien muss sterbien" (Serbia must die) and "Jeder Russ ein Schuss, jeder Franzos ein Stoss, jeder Britt ein Tritt" (a shot for every Russian, a shove for every Frenchman, a kick for every Briton); "Scherflein beitragen" (do one's bit) and "Nibelungentreue" (the troth of the Nibelungs, meaning Austro-German unity); "Gott strafe England" (God punish England) and "Gold gab ich für Eisen" (I gave gold in return for iron—to help the Austrian war effort).[14]

Street-corner chauvinists threaten a Serbian barber as well as an American mistaken for an Englishman, two Chinese mistaken for Japanese, and a Turk who speaks French. The "little people" deface store inscriptions containing French and English words; the name of the Café Westminster offends the xenophobic crowd, yet "Cafe Westmünster" will do. (Later, the dishes served at a restaurant are Germanized: *oeufs pochées* have become *verlorene Eier* and *Makkaroni* appears as *Treubruchnudeln,* or perfidy noodles.) Yet the language of these patriots and purists is studded with "enemy" words like *tuschiert, odios, replizieren, echauffieren, apropos,* and *fisafis.* The military cliché "einrückend machen" (mobilize or activate), used over and over again, reflects the degradation of the individual and the obliteration of his personality. The *Ausputzen* (cleaning out) of enemy trenches is one of many locutions indicating that language has gone to war and is engaged in a life-and-death struggle. A reporter describes the mood of the people as "far from arrogance and weakness . . . proud of feeling on their own bodies the pulse of the great times now dawning"; there is "a southern capacity for enthusiasm, guided and controlled by German serious-ness." [15] Readers of the *Reichspost* say that "wars are processes of purification, seedbeds of virtue, and arousers of heroes" and that the war will "bring about a renascence of Austrian thought and action." [16]

In the first of their many conversations (there are three in each of the first three acts, six in Act Four and eight in Act Five), the *Nörgler* (Grumbler or Faultfinder) tells the Optimist that in wartime servants have power and everyone becomes the superior of his fellow man. When the Optimist asks "Don't you see that a new, a great era has dawned?", the Grumbler replies, "I knew it when it was this small, and it will become so again." [17] The Grumbler is, of course, Karl Kraus himself, and the Optimist, a figure possibly inspired by the politician Heinrich Lammasch (whom Kraus esteemed and who became Austria's prime Minister at the very end of the war), may be regarded as a composite of all enlightened and humane but naïve and temporarily misguided Austrians. "I like to converse with you," says the Grumbler in one of their later conversations; "you supply the cues for my monologues." [18]

These dialogues—the choruses of the tragedy, as it were—are oases of relative repose and reflection; sometimes political conclusions are reached from satirical premises. In his running commentary, the Grumbler constitutes the voice of reason; presenting eschatological views rather than historicism or *Realpolitik,* he alone displays the kind of awareness and intellectual consistency that might have saved European civilization. *Nörgler* Kraus is the everpresent, increasingly anguished conscience in the play. (In Scene 25, to be sure, a speculator and a real-estate owner agree that "Fackelkraus" has disappeared and must be all written out; his satires were fun in peacetime, but no one is in the mood for them now).[19]

Scene 29, one of the longer conversations between the Optimist and the Grumbler, contains a powerful and sustained diatribe against the

Germanic spirit. In representing the idea that God did not create man as a consumer or producer but as a human being, Kraus calls the Chinese the only race sufficiently strong and moral to survive technology and remain unaffected by this dealers' war serving militarism and materialism, "the idea of the Jewish-capitalistic destruction of the world." [20] When the Optimist refers to the Germans by the time-honored designation "Volk der Dichter und Denker" (nation of poets and thinkers), the Grumbler makes the sardonic pun "Volk der Richter und Henker" (nation of judges and hangmen).[21] "No nation" he says, "is so alienated from its language, and therefore from the source of its very life, as the Germans." [22] The Grumbler finds the combination of heroism and business particularly odious. In this war, he feels, culture does not renew itself but saves itself from the hangman by committing suicide. It is more than sin: daily lies from which printer's ink flows like blood. This war cannot be ended by a peace but only by a war of the universe against this planet gone stark raving mad. For someone like the Grumbler there is only this last moral duty: "to sleep unfeelingly through this anxious waiting period until he is redeemed by the word, or by God's impatience." [23]

This may have been the Grumbler's wish, but it could not be Kraus's reality; the evidences of man's betrayal of the spirit were too prevalent and cried out for documentation and artistic exposure. There was the Bavarian storyteller Ludwig Ganghofer, immensely popular with the masses—especially the rural population—who yodelled his way along the front, wrote war reports for the *Neue Freie Presse,* and swapped stories with an appreciative Kaiser Wilhelm. There was Conrad von Hötzendorf, the Austrian chief of staff, who posed for photographers while studying maps. There was Alice Schalek, the first woman correspondent accredited to the Austrian army, whose gushy effusions in a denatured language about "the common man," "the liberated human spirit," and "the fever of experiencing", whose constant search for "atmosphere," "contrasts," the "sensations" of men in battle, and other "human-interest" material amidst death and destruction made her a macabre joke and a frequent target of Kraus's satire.[24] There was the guiding spirit of the *Neue Freie Presse,* Moriz Benedikt, whose influential position as the dean of Austrian journalism entitled him to Kraus's mordant appellation "lord of the hyenas." [25]

In one of many instances in which successive scenes underline ironies or reinforce incongruities, Scenes 27 and 28 are, so to speak, a juxtaposition of a benediction and a "benedictation." At the Vatican, the praying Pope Benedict XV implores the governments to end the fighting and the carnage; in his office, the dictating Moriz Benedikt delivers himself of some tastelessly morbid remarks about fishes and other denizens of the Adriatic Sea which are now enjoying feasts because of all those sunk ships. At a time when "newspapers have served for the lighting of a world conflagration . . . what chance does a sermon for peace have against an editorial for war? . . . Bethlehem in America is correcting the mistake that was made 1900 years ago. Bethlehem is the name of the biggest cannon foundry in the United States." [26]

Seemingly trivial but equally symptomatic of the world conflagration, the rape of language, the perversion of cultural values, and the betrayal of the spirit is a phenomenon that was to become an obsession with Kraus. In Scene 13 of Act Two, he presents two *Hofräte* (privy councilors) who are eager to publish their adaptations of Goethe's immortal poem "Über allen Gipfeln ist Ruh" ("Over all the hilltops it is quiet"). In this case, the "Wanderers Nachtlied" ("Wanderer's Night Song") has become the "Wanderers Schlachtlied" ("Wanderer's Battle Chant"): "Hindenburg is asleep in the forest; wait, soon Warsaw too will fall." [27] In another version, *"Ruh"* is changed to "U" for U-boat; as in an unwitting panegyric of submarine warfare a British captain comments lyrically on the sinking of his ship, and "of England's fleet you can feel hardly a breath." [28] "While cozily reaching for death-dealing machines," says the Grumbler, "today's beasts also reach for verses to glorify them." [29]

At the beginning of Act Two, the question is raised whether two organisms can be imagined as standing "shoulder to shoulder . . . when the very substance of one is based on disorder and only its inefficiency has kept it from disintegrating, and when the other organism consists of, and exists by, nothing but order." [30] Austro-German understanding is illustrated by the exasperation of a war profiteer from Berlin at his failure to make a Viennese type understand his German; he, in turn, takes the latter's dialect to be English.

In Scene 27, an Austrian general at the Uzsok Pass tells his officers that in the next war Austrian organization must be better; a Prussian lieutenant boorishly barges into the room and barks at the general because the Austrians cannot handle the Uzsok situation by themselves, whereupon the Austrian makes an admiring remark on the Germans' dash and organizing talent. The second pair of discussants in the play, the *Abonnent* (Newspaper Subscriber) and the Patriot display the wholly predictable mentality of those nurtured upon the propaganda of a corrupt government and the effusions of a mendacious and meretricious press. One of Kraus's fictitious characters, Old Biach, literally dies of linguistic convolution when even he can no longer reconcile the reality of the breakdown with journalistic double-talk and patriotic double-think. Part of this mentality is a sentimental attachment to Emperor Franz Joseph, and several scenes feature Ralph Benatzky's popular song about the "guater alter Herr in Schönbrunn," the "good old gentleman in Schönbrunn," of whom Kraus had become increasingly critical.[31]

The temper of the times is further illustrated by the gaping multitudes visiting the exhibit of a real trench in the Prater; by a field chaplain of the "praise-the-Lord-and-pass-the-ammunition" variety; by a suburban crowd threatening an old lady who had protested against the use of half-starved dogs to pull a cart; by a soldier-father chastising his half-starved boy who had dared to ask for a hot breakfast; by the owner of a factory under the military-service law who keeps a whip in readiness for union agitators; by the social climbing of a Jewish couple named Schwarz-Gelber (after the colors of the monarchy, black and yellow); by the military commander, Archduke Friedrich, soon to receive an honorary doctorate from the University of Vienna, who may or may not have been the one who acknowledged the mortar fire seen and heard on a movie screen with a viscerally onomatopoetic, very Austrian *"Bumsti!"* (Wham!). "You make it hard for a man to be an optimist," the Grumbler is told; "your method is discoloring all flags of the fatherland. Everything is lies and prostitution? Where is truth?" "Among the prostitutes."[32]

In Act Three the accustomed cry of a newspaper vendor, "Extraausgabee—!", which Mary Snell has described as "a kind of sardonic trumpet alarm,"[33] and the ritualized opening *danse macabre* of automata are followed by a bit of front-line "atmosphere" and war humor (the Katzelmacher March sung on the Isonzo front: "Tschiff, tscheff, tauch, der Wallisch liegt am Bauch"[34] [Whiz, bang, whack, the wop's flat on his back]). Two students of philosophy in Jena applaud the hawkish machinations of their professors; a Viennese grocer jacks up his prices and barks at his cowed customers; at a Berlin chemical laboratory, Professor Delbrück claims that the population fares better than ever on *ersatz* foodstuffs. While upper-class Jewish society, surrounded by beggars and cripples, carries on as usual, the Cherusker, a superpatriotic, nationalistic, anti-Semitic group of self-styled Teutons, meet at Krems; at a German playground marked "No Admittance to Wounded Soldiers" children play *Weltkrieg* (World War), the latest war game (their father has invented it and others, such as "Distribution of the Booty" and "Russian Death" as well as sentimental artifacts like "Hero's Grave in the Home"); other children mouth the language of war communiqués and slogans like "A Place in the Sun."

After two men are shown on their way to the war ministry to "sichs richten," to "fix it" for themselves, fifty draft dodgers point at one another, saying *"He* ought to be inducted!"[35]; a civilian trying to find out the fate of his missing son is told by a captain whose office hours are over to go ahead and assume that his son is dead, and anyway, "it's best to die for the Fatherland." At several churches, patriotic sermons are preached: killing is a Christian duty and a deeply religious act; if thousands have been maimed and blinded, God wanted to save their souls that way. At a Roman Catholic pilgrimage church, where the bell is about to be made into a cannon, there is a special display piece: a rosary made of Italian shrapnel, barbed wire, and grenades.

Discussing chemical and bacterial warfare, the Grumbler draws a parallel between the old Hebrews and the Germans; the former heeded the commandment "Thou shalt not kill," while the modern Germans interpret Kant's categorical imperative as a philosophical justification for "Immer feste druff" (Up and at 'em!).[36] At the Austrian War Archives, literary figures like Rilke, Robert Müller, Werfel, Felix Dörmann, and Hans Müller are shown writing martial poems, feuilletons, captions, and reports to order. Hans Müller reports about his wonderful experiences and encounters in the "grosse Zeit," and as he fabricates reports from the front while safe in Vienna, he is received at the Hofburg by the grateful German Kaiser. At a Berlin lecture hall, Richard Dehmel reads one of his chauvinistic war poems to great applause, and at a newspaper office in the same city Alfred Kerr is shown working on his brutally parodistic *Rumänenlied (Rumanian Song)*, while the Styrian priest Ottokar Kernstock concocts his bloodthirsty rhymes. By contrast, Kraus depicts himself reading his poem "Mit der Uhr in der Hand" ("With Watch in Hand", about a U-boat sinking a troop transport in forty-three seconds) at a Vienna lecture hall. A drunk urinating on the street next to the column memorializing the plague on Vienna's Graben becomes for Kraus the indestructible memorial of his time.

In keeping with the declining fortunes of the war, gaiety alternates with sullen silence among the "ghouls and lemures" introducing Act

Four. The dramatic typology of man's inhumanity to man continues: a commander gives orders to sacrifice four thousand troops in a pointless offensive on the Russian front and then orders the chastisement of hungry men attempting to buy food; at a military hospital, wounded men beg for silence, but, of course, the field marshal cannot do without his gay dinner music; German and Bulgarian editors in Sofia discuss "British envy, French vengefulness, and Russian rapacity";[3][7] the age of minors convicted by a military tribunal is given as twenty-one so that the death sentence can be carried out; a military judge named Zagorski is proud of his anniversary: he has pronounced 110 death sentences and personally attended every execution; in the Carpathian Mountains a sadistic commander maltreats soldiers and then writes a sanctimonious letter to the father of a man whom he has tortured to death; at a Weimar women's clinic, Professor Henkel performs a needless operation to provide a spectacle for a visiting prince; and Kaiser Wilhelm performs various vulgar tricks for his sycophantic officers. At a doctors' meeting in Berlin, a psychiatrist discusses a "madman" with pacifist convictions who has doubts about Germany's victory. The man challenges Dr. Boas to deny that eight hundred thousand people have starved, that in the first half of 1918 70 per cent more Germans died of tuberculosis than in all of 1913. Convinced that the man is not only insane but in the pay of the Entente, the psychiatrist has him arrested as a criminal.

In a long conversation in Scene 29, the Optimist claims that the entire drama arose from the Grumbler's unhappy penchant for combining trivial occurrences with historical events. The Grumbler makes the point that his patriotism, being different from that of the "patriots," does not permit him to let a satirist from an enemy country do the job; he would advise an English satirist to concern himself with the affairs of his own country. To the Optimist's statement that "the Austro-Hungarian monarchy is a historical necessity," the Grumbler replies:

Maybe, because all this national variety-store stuff which has plunged us into cultural disgrace and material misery must be kept in some accursed corner of the world. But this necessity will grow weaker with all revolutionary and martial attempts to get rid of it, and if this cannot be done, if the royal-imperial idea turns out to be ineradicable, there will be more wars. For reasons of prestige this monarchy ought to have committed suicide long ago.[3][8]

The Grumbler inveighs against Franz Joseph, a man held up to him as a great and universally admired monarch: "Never before in world history has a stronger non-personality put his stamp on all things and forms, so that in everything blocking our path, in all miseries and communication breakdowns, at the bottom of every misfortune we spotted this imperial beard. . . . A demon of mediocrity had decided our destiny." [39] He speaks of "Habsburg's scepter whose mission it seemed to be to hover over world peace as a Damoclean sword . . . this Franz Joseph who was spared nothing but a personality." [40] The latter reference is to a favorite locution of the Emperor: "Mir bleibt doch nichts erspart" (I am spared nothing). This phrase, along with another trite favorite, "Es was sehr schön, es hat mich sehr gefreut" (It was very nice, I enjoyed it very much), is featured in a couplet with many "Katastrophen" (cata-strophes) which Kraus has the Emperor, "the Habsburg demon incarnate," [41] sing in his sleep in a later scene, [42] which was written in 1915, the year before Franz Joseph's death. *Nörgler* Kraus reveals that he took his drama to Switzerland to put the finishing touches to it there; thanks to Austrian *Schlamperei* (sloppiness) it passed the border inspection twice. Another prime exhibit in Kraus's indictment of his time is discussed in the same conversation: the photograph (widely circulated as a picture postcard) on which the hanged corpse of Cesare Battisti, a South Tyrolean who had collaborated with the Italians, is flanked by the grinning or smug faces of his hangman and the Austrian officers and civilians who were jostling one another to get into the picture. (This is one of two pictures which Kraus used to illustrate his play.)

The slightly surrealistic setting at the beginning of Act Five ("Wet and cold. It is raining from below. A mutely staring herd of rams. Cordon of wounded and dead")[43] is rendered realistic by the insipid talk of playboy officers and the voice of a coachman: "In wartime I get fifty times as much!" [44] A rally for a German peace produces slogans like "Down with world conscience and international brotherhood! . . . More German power!" [45] A dissident who says that the moral corrosion of the body politic by trickery and thievery can never be gilded by the glory of arms is ejected, and Professor Puppe proceeds to make impudent demands of Germany's foes. A conversation between the Subscriber and the Patriot produces hilarious semantic variations on the theme of the *Ausbau* (consolidation) and *Vertiefung* (deepening) of the Austro-German alliance. At a battlefield near Saarburg, Major Metzler (Massacre) and Captain Niedermacher (Downmower) agree that no prisoners should be taken; they are to be killed on higher orders. (Similar sentiments are expressed in the next scene, set near Verdun, by

French officers named Gloirefaisant, Meurtrier, and De Massacré.) At a
café on the Ringstrasse there is a fauna of figures swapping trading lore;
these men bear not only the animal names commonly used by
Jews—Löw, Hirsch, Wolf—but also such names as Mammut, Zieselmaus,
Walross, Hamster, Nashorn, Tapir, Schakal, Leguan, Kaimann, Pavian,
Kondor, Mastodon. An old profiteer suffers a breakdown: he has heard
a rumor that peace may break out! In Scene 28, Grumbler Kraus is
shown reciting his "Prayer" in a Vienna lecture hall:

> Almighty God, avert these eyes of mine!
> Grant me a merciful forgetting,
> lest I must witness how they take to wine
> as mock replacement for the blood they're letting.
>
> Almighty God, dispel this evil day!
> Take back to childhood me in kindness.
> The end is still so very far away,
> so strike me—like those conquerors—with blindness.
>
> Almighty God, so let my tongue go numb!
> Keep me from mouthing their expressions.
> They make themselves not only dead but dumb,
> with Truth the victim of their hate-obsessions.
>
> Almighty God, creator of the thought—
> they killed it off by their conniving,
> Their word has turned all earthly worth to naught,
> with neither deeds nor even Death surviving.
>
> Almighty God, obstruct my ears as well!
> The music's pitch is climbing higher.
> Poor Satan got the shivers down in Hell—
> Now he feels cozy in this cannon fire.
>
> Almighty God, Who gave the living breath
> to men of science and invention:
> that they should pay You back by dealing death
> with toxic gases—was that Your intention?
>
> Almighty God, why did You call me here
> at just this time, so Godforsaken?
> You smite with famine, yet the profiteer
> enjoys his meal unpunished and unshaken.
>
> Almighty God, why did it have to be
> this era and this blood arena
> where he who still lives on sits down with glee
> to feast upon the dead like a hyena?

> Almighty God, this country is a scroll
> on which with blood they are inscribing
> their merry parties. Murder pays the toll . . .
> Their gags make grief the object of their gibing.
>
> Almighty God, did You perhaps in rage
> create the vampire generation?
> Then save me from this breed and from this age,
> this parasites-and-hangmen type of nation!
>
> Almighty God, find me a land on earth
> where money is no cause of dying,
> And where man's heritage is human worth—
> not ill-won riches, decency defying.
>
> Almighty God, have You no means at all
> to stop these robot politicians
> who, fearing not the final trumpet call,
> pursue their war with cannons and commissions?
>
> Almighty God, remove me from this scheme
> and from this bloodstained path I tread on.
> Convert this nightmare into just a dream,
> a vision of Your coming Armageddon![4][6]

This is followed by applause and a listener's remark to his wife: "Well, you should know that he once tried to get on the staff of the *Neue Freie Presse*." [4][7]

Scene 54 consists of a long soliloquy by the Grumbler sitting at his desk:

Why was I not given the strength to mow down the sin of this planet with one blow of an axe? Why did I not have the mental power to force an outcry out of desecrated mankind? I am preserving documents for an age which will no longer comprehend or will be so far removed from today that it will call me a fabricator. . . . I have written a tragedy whose falling hero is mankind, whose tragic conflict, the conflict between the world and nature, has a fatal ending. . . . I have taken upon myself the tragedy, which breaks down into the scenes of mankind breaking down, so that it may be heard by the spirit which takes pity on victims.[4][8]

As the tragedy rushes toward its apocalyptic end, two fat Berlin profiteers named Gog and Magog disport themselves in the snow in the Swiss Alps; a woman writes to her soldier-husband that she is carrying another man's child; ragged remnants of regiments are dressed up to make an impression on the visiting emperor; prisoners of war are brutalized at every turn; heroism is exploited commercially and theatrically; and a deserted street eerily reverberates with the cries of newspaper hawkers, "corybants and maenads" spewing forth word fragments ("It sounds as though the woe of mankind were being dredged up from a deep well").[49]

"This war will not end with a peace," says the Grumbler. "It did not take place on the surface of life, but raged within life itself. The front has extended into the hinterland.... The world is going under, and no one will know it. Forgotten will be all that happened yesterday; what happens today will not be noticed; no one will fear what is due tomorrow. It will be forgotten that the war was lost, forgotten that the war was started, forgotten that it was waged. For that reason the war will never stop..."[50]

The long final scene is a dance on a volcano. Against the backdrop of a huge mural entitled "Die grosse Zeit," Austrian and Prussian officers feast at a banquet, carousing, singing, and flirting vulgarly against the counterpoint of bad war news coming in. The general's drunkenly dialectal observation "Durch san's"[51] (They've broken through) is the signal for a tableau of many rapidly shifting apparitions, a cluster of apocalyptic scenes depicting the horrors of war: Half-starved children scavenging for food find shrapnels which explode; other children play with hanged men; a soldier senselessly stabs a shepherd dog and an officer, equally senselessly, shoots a waitress; a hospital ship is sunk. There are choruses of Gas Masks, Frozen Soldiers, Flames, 1200 Drowned Horses, the Doomed Children on the *Lusitania*, Army Dogs, Ravens, Camp Followers, an Unborn Son. This phantasmagoric sequence—and the play—conclude with a wall of flames on the horizon and screams of death outside.

III   "Die letzte Nacht"

The rhymed Epilogue "Die letzte Nacht" ("The Last Night") is a harrowing poetic satire raised to a supernatural plane. In it Kraus recapitulates many motifs of his play in concentrated, cinematographic form, with actual and allegorical characters appearing in a ghastly operatic procession. A moribund soldier screams that he is not dying for any emperor or fatherland; male and female gas masks discuss their sexlessness and facelessness; a general riding over corpses in his flight intones a *Sprechgesang:* even a dead corporal must observe dress regulations. A war correspondent asks a soldier who is bleeding to death to look "transfigured"; he cannot take him to a hospital because he needs to record the exact moment at which his eye breaks. Having reached the soldier before his death, the newspapermen feel they have a right to his last "sensations" and only regret that there is no chaplain to administer the last rites in their presence.

Other revolting specimens of *homo sapiens* include a dashing hussar; the martial Nowotny von Eichensieg, who traffics in "human material," and the scientist Dr. Siegfried Abendrot, master of chemical warfare and inventor of the *Lungenpestersatz*, a subtle poison working on the lungs. The human hyenas Fressack (Glutton) and Naschkatz (Sweet-tooth), representing the parasitic commercial, industrial, and journal-istic interests of the war, are followed by the Lord of the Hyenas (Moriz Benedikt). A typology of troops gives way to a dramatic confrontation between Voices from Above and Voices from Below, with the higher voices speaking truth and the lower ones mouthing the falsehoods of the "great times." "Wir haben alles reiflich erwogen" [52] (We have carefully considered everything), says the last Voice from Above in an adaptation of the late emperor's statement.

After a stinging indictment of this planet, a shower of meteors, accompanied by cosmic thunder, incinerates the earth. "God's image" is destroyed, and following a great silence the closing Voice of God speaks the words of Kaiser Wilhelm II at the beginning of the war: "Ich habe es nicht gewollt" [53] (I did not want it). As Max Spalter has pointed out, "Kraus's God is . . . the Judaeo-Christian God and can only weep at what man has brought on himself." [54] Since a God of love and goodness desired neither chaos nor apocalypse, there remains a final glimmer of hope—one expressed by Kraus the poet rather than Kraus the satirist—that man will yet redeem himself and work toward a better destiny.

IV   Weltgericht

The fact that Kraus was able to write *Die letzten Tage der Menschheit* as well as publish and recite large portions of his pacifist play in wartime may be regarded as evidence that the "last days of mankind" were perhaps not even the penultimate days; as compared to the later course of world history, they were relatively benign ones. Kraus's epigram "Satires which the censor understands are rightly prohibited" [55] does not tell the whole story. Part of the evidence is the continued publication of *Die Fackel* during the war, although sections of it did run afoul of censorship and were suppressed. *Weltgericht*, a two-volume compilation of material published in the *Fackel* between

1914 and 1919, is a sort of pacifist primer, an effusion from the same bitter brew that produced *Die letzten Tage der Menschheit.*

In the last year of the war, the government started proceedings against Kraus because of the supposed corrosive, defeatist, and treasonous tendency of his writings and public lectures. In the title essay, written in October, 1918, Kraus refers to the two thousand pages of the wartime *Fackel* as "a fraction of what technical and governmental obstacles have limited me to." [56] Earlier, in "The Serious Times and the Satire of Earlier Days" (1915), he had written: "I am not so cowardly as to fight censorship. I am courageous enough to give way to it." [57] In the face of the shattering stability of those phenomena which had provided the raw material for his satire in the past fifteen years, he was not minded to express any retroactive regrets that he processed this material or that *Die Fackel* had continued to appear. His was the greater courage: to see the enemy in his own camp: "I declare that I regard the wildest procession of freed slaves as a more orderly spectacle and one more pleasing in the sight of God than the official death march of human cattle for someone else's idiocy and crime." [58] In this polluted patriotic air, Kraus says, he has moved only with his eyes open and his nose shut. "How despicable yesterday's openers of carriage doors look as builders of barricades. . . . Henceforth I shall never be able to speak with a good-natured, foul-smelling, blear-eyed bookkeeper, because he would suddenly start telling me about his exploits in Belgrade." [59]

Weltgericht (Last Judgment) ranges from "In dieser grossen Zeit" (December, 1914) to "Nachruf" (January, 1919). The final "Epitaph" is a long tour de force. What sustained men like Kraus in the night of nights while they were cold and hungry and dragged themselves toward a peaceful day when the necessities of life would no longer pose an intellectual problem and constitute the substance of one's existence, was the thought that they would no longer be Austrians. But this experience was marred for them by the fact that the new state bore a name which would recall to the world the hated Central Powers, not to mention memories of a hell extending over centuries.

Kraus was disappointed at the continued existence of "this bureaucratic nightmare of scenic beauty . . . this dissolved association of jovial executioners . . . this improbable fatherland which sent its martyrs off to a war which it knew to be lost . . . this Satanic idea of a state whose existence ran counter to all claims of physical and moral purity." [60] On no side were the principles of international legal norms more flagrantly violated than on the German side—because of a whole army of journalistic, literary, and academic rogues that accused the other side of inhuman warfare and then applauded the bombing of hospitals, churches, and schools. Yet this epitaph for war criminals and their victims in Germany and Austria culminates in an optimism which seems almost naïve today. "The individual nations ought to forget," wrote Kraus; "but let mankind forget and forgive none of what it has done to itself." [61] *Die Dritte Walpurgisnacht,* written less than a decade and a half later, seems like a horrible, delayed epilogue to this epitaph. And the undiminished validity of *Die letzten Tage der Menschheit* is evident as well, even to Kraus's detractors. As Mary Snell (an appreciative critic) has put it, "Fifty years after Kraus wrote his monster-satire his words are as dramatically intense and as alive as on the day when they were still news." [62]

CHAPTER 6

The Unconquerable

An individual cannot help an epoch or save
it; he can only express that it is going
to ruin.

—Kierkegaard, 1849

I *Ghosts in the Land*

THE STORY of Kraus's postwar writings and polemics is basically the history of his postwar disillusionment as his "homeland's loyal hater."[1] In "After Twenty Years," a poem written on the twentieth anniversary of the *Fackel* in 1919, Kraus enumerated his themes—past, present, and future—"Sex and untruth, stupidity, abuses, cadences and clichés, ink, technology, death, war and society, usury, politics, the insolence of office and the spurns that patient merit of the unworthy takes, art and nature, love and dreams. . . ."[2] The best Kraus could say about the Austrian Republic was that it had replaced the monarchy. In an extended and brilliant response to a letter from Karl Seitz, the prominent Social Democratic politician, Chairman of the National Assembly and subsequent mayor of Vienna, who had congratulated Kraus on the twentieth anniversary of the *Fackel* and acknowledged his contribution toward the exorcism of old ghosts, he wrote:

There is nothing to be more greatly feared than ghosts which have been chased away and are still there. For as long as we have the journalists, we shall have them all. They have all been attracted by the black magic which, in accordance with my prediction, has brought about the destruction of the world. There always is a bit of spirit left, a piece of nature which they could kill for us by drawing it into their unspeakable element. . . . What one wishes for the Republic is that it may make an end of the parasites remaining from the imperial age as well as the comedos of the revolution, that male pride may finally assert itself before publishers' thrones and break the machines of an industry which, under the depraved pretense of freedom of the press, is leading a nation to its death with its lies. . . . Only then will the ghosts have been driven out.[3]

The ghosts were still around and as elusive as ever. How was Kraus, for example, to deal with the ghastly mentality displayed by a Basel newspaper in 1921 which offered, as he put it, "Reklamefahrten zur Hölle" (Promotional Trips to Hell)—round trips to the battle-fields *par excellence* of Verdun, "at reduced rates, first-class accommodations and food, tips included"?[4] Kraus likened his situation in postwar Austria to Peer Gynt's struggle with the Great Boyg—"the Boyg does not fight—and does not lose."[5] In an epigram entitled "Das Hiesige," he writes: "You call out to it and it's gone . . . you touch air . . . abysses wherever you go . . . everything resists without resistance . . . as it gives way, you are defeated . . . no matter what I did and said: It was too soft, it did not yield!"[6] For this reason he felt impelled to keep redefining his mission. Kraus repeatedly had occasion to remark that the age recognized itself too easily in his material and was blind to the artistic elements he had wrested from it. In 1919 he wrote: "Only my tenacity, which does not want to miss even the smallest occasion for demonstrating the world's ills, keeps pushing me into contact with an incurable world."[7] Above all, Kraus did not wish to be regarded as a mere polemicist.

> I abhor such a hero and can only abide
> Expressing in verse how I feel:
> He is like Siegfried with his thick hide,
> Like Achilles with his heel.[8]

"A polemic is an unauthorized action which, in exceptional cases, becomes mandatory for a personality", he wrote. "I regard polemics which are not art as breaches of social tact which make people feel sympathy for the evil object."[9] A seeming paradox is contained in an aphoristic statement from *Nachts:* "The comprehension of my work is made more difficult by knowledge of my material. People do not see that what exists first has to be invented and that it is worth inventing, nor do they understand that a satirist for whom persons exist in such a way as though he had invented them needs more strength than one who invents persons as though they were there."[10] In an epigram entitled "Glosses Become Symbols" as well as in a poem Kraus describes his own situation and pinpoints what impedes his full effectiveness:

> Only those distant in time or space
> Can know my satire's true face.
> Neighbor Meyer sees my outlook worsen,
> Because he knows Herr Mueller in person.[11]

Here In This Land

Here in this land no one is deemed absurd,
but who should speak the truth. And all defenseless
he stands before the sneering grinning herd,
who hold a sense of honor senseless.

Here in this land, where God is bought and sold
and manhood is pursued with execration,
all infamy is coined to purest gold
and lords it high in honor's station.

Here in this land you run a gauntlet's lane
of cut-purses who fervently despise you
and either get your purse by some chicane
or slap your back to show they prize you.

Here in this land, whatever be your boast,
you are not master of your own decision.
The pest of greed obtrudes by every post,
effectively to blight your vision.

Here in this land you beat the empty air
when you denounce one evil or another,
and every grinning rascal debonair
in this land hails you as his brother.[1][2]

II *Friends and Foes, Apostles and Apostates*

Kraus appeared to his contemporaries, by turns, as a prophetic thinker, a passionate Jewish prophet in the Old Testament sense, a pacifist in the spirit of Christianity, a well-intentioned educator, a benign sponsor of young or neglected poets, a social revolutionary, a conservative guardian of the German and Austrian tradition, an exalted model, a sadistic slanderer, and a cynical mocker of all values. To some he was a breathtaking incarnation of the absolute, an infallible oracle, a prophet desperately trying to show mankind the right way by pointing it back to the "origin" which, to him, was forever the goal; to others, he was an embittered, monomaniacal misanthrope, a man who directed his cannon fire at sparrows, an object of fear, vituperation, and blind hatred. This ambivalence is seen in Kraus's relationship to some of his contemporaries, for in a number of instances apostles turned apostates, disciples became defectors, friends changed to foes, and those once championed were later chastised. Only relatively few disciples had the strength of character and the absolute integrity that Kraus demanded of them. More often than not, such falls from grace took place under unedifying circumstances and had both personal and literary repercussions, sometimes leading to acrimonious polemics and public pillorying.

Kraus's splendid isolation precluded any idea of a "circle" forming around him, but it is not hard to compile a list of creative men and women who were close to him in an atmosphere of mutual respect and admiration. Peter Altenberg and Adolf Loos were among Kraus's oldest friends. Kraus not only was instrumental in launching Altenberg's literary career by gathering his scattered manuscripts and sending them to a prominent publisher, who brought out Altenberg's first collection *Wie ich es sehe,* but on numerous occasions he wrote appreciatively about his friend, recited from his works, aided the indigent writer financially, eulogized him at his funeral, and in 1932 edited an Altenberg anthology. The architect Adolf Loos and Kraus were kindred spirits, and Kraus spoke moving words at Loos's funeral in 1933. "All that Adolf Loos and I did—he literally, I linguistically," he once wrote, "was to show that there is a difference between an urn and a chamber pot, and that in this difference there is leeway for culture. But the others, the 'positive ones,' are divided into those who use the urn as a chamberpot and those who use the chamberpot as an urn." [13]

Kraus's championship of the German-Jewish poetess Else Lasker-Schüler was based on his conviction not only of her literary talent but of her uncompromising stand as a high priestess of poetry and her linguistic-moral truthfulness. Kraus helped her in many ways, including the collection of funds. The correspondence between these very dissimilar spirits extended from 1909 to 1924. Else Lasker-Schüler characteristically addressed Kraus as "Duke of Vienna," "Cardinal," or "Dalai Lama." Her last words addressed to him in their correspondence, *"Ich hasse Sie"* [14] (I hate you), should not be taken as evidence of a complete break but must be read in the context of the life and work of the eccentric poetess. [15]

Kraus's literary and personal appreciation of writers and artists like Detlev von Liliencron, Otto Weininger, Frank Wedekind, August Strindberg, Oscar Wilde, Franz Janowitz, Franz Grüner, Karl Hauer, and Oskar Kokoschka is fully documented in his writings. Other literary figures who came under his spell were Franz Werfel, Felix Salten, Willy Haas, Fritz Wittels, and Albert Ehrenstein (all later "apostates"), Ludwig Thoma, Otto Stoessl, Andreas Latzko, Otto Soyka, Alfred Polgar, Egon Friedell, Friedrich Torberg, Sigismund von Radecki, Paul Engelmann, and—last not least—his biographers Robert Scheu, Leopold Liegler, Berthold Viertel, and Heinrich Fischer.

Kraus also treasured the friendship of Ludwig von Janikowski (the inspirer of *Sittlichkeit und Kriminalität* and the first to recognize in Kraus's work "the intellectual perspective of those trivia which the blind mistake for the substance" [16]), Prince Max Lobkowitz, Karl Jaray, and the art historian Ludwig Münz. The gifted women to whom he felt attached included—in addition to Annie Kalmar, Sidonie Nadherny, Elisabeth Reitler, and Helen Kann—Countess Mary Dobrzensky and the poet, essayist, storyteller, and composer Mechtilde Lichnowsky.

In addition to the accompanists at Kraus's recitals, there was a relationship of mutual admiration with the musicians Ernst Křenek, Arnold Schönberg, Eduard Steuermann, Alban Berg, and Rudolf Kolisch. Heinrich Lammasch, Thomas Masaryk, and Friedrich Austerlitz were among the political leaders whom Kraus admired. He had a close working and human relationship with his attorney Oskar Samek, his printers Georg and Martin Jahoda, and Richard Lanyi, the bookdealer and sometime publisher whose shop on Kärntnerstrasse became a headquarters for Krausians, where his works as well as tickets to his recitals were sold. Mutual respect bound Kraus to the circle around the periodical *Der Brenner,* published at Innsbruck and often favorably mentioned by Kraus: to its longtime editor Ludwig von Ficker, the poet Georg Trakl, and the philosophers and scholars Theodor Haecker, Carl Dallago, Karl Borromäus Heinrich, and Ferdinand Ebner—Catholic thinkers who appreciated Kraus's eschatological orientation.

The German-Jewish publicist Maximilian Harden, born in 1861, was a mentor of the young Kraus, and *Die Fackel* was patterned in part on Harden's periodical *Die Zukunft.* The first volumes of the *Fackel* contain a number of appreciative comments on Harden (then not yet "Herr Harden," "Herr" being an appellation used as part of Kraus's satiric technique). In 1903 Kraus noted with some displeasure that Harden had published an essay in the *Neue Freie Presse* and found occasion to disagree with Harden's view that the Viennese press was superior to Berlin journalism. Kraus soon saw a parting of the ways in Harden's views on the Hervay trial and the case of Princess Louise von Coburg, an attitude that differed markedly from Kraus's stand in the *Sittlichkeit und Kriminalität* essays. Harden tried to fight the Wilhelminian regime by exposing the homosexuality rampant in the "court camarilla," involving himself in suits against Prince Philipp zu Eulenburg and Count Kuno Moltke. In a number of *Fackel* essays (later included in *Die chinesische Mauer* and *Literatur und Lüge*) Kraus inveighed against Harden's mentality ("I have a hatred in my heart and feverishly await the opportunity to release it")[17]

Characteristically, the language of the man whom Kraus had earlier called a great essayist was taken as an index of this snooper's unworthiness. Kraus repeatedly printed "translations" from what he called Harden's "Desperanto" as well as "Harden Lexica" illuminating Harden's baroque locutions and euphuisms.[18] The polemic was exacerbated by Harden's public reply in 1906 in which he alluded to Kraus's *"grotesker Roman"* (grotesque novel or romance) with Annie Kalmar. This seemed particularly reprehensible to Kraus because of Harden's firsthand knowledge as his trusted confidant at the time ("Herr Harden is dead—the grotesque novel lives . . . and I believe I owe my best to it").[19] Harden lived until 1927, having stopped publication of *Die Zukunft* in 1922, following a physical attack upon him. In an obituary article, Franz Pfemfert said that shortly before his death Harden had expressed himself very favorably on Kraus.[20]

The psychoanalyst Fritz Wittels published some essays in the early *Fackel* under the pseudonym Avicenna. In 1908 Kraus printed a series of aphorisms dealing with the disloyalty which he was experiencing in some cases and foreseeing in others. Wittels may have been offended by a veiled allusion to him, for in 1910 he published a novel entitled *Ezechiel der Zugereiste (Ezechiel the Newcomer)* in which Kraus appears as Benjamin Eckelhaft (Nassty), editor of *Das Riesenmaul (The Giant Mouth)*. Another portrait of Kraus is given in the story of Ernesto, an exhibitionist with "hysterogenic complexes," which is included in Wittels' book *Alles um Liebe,* published in 1912. On January 12, 1910, Wittels presented a paper on "The *Fackel* Neurosis" at a meeting of the Vienna Psychoanalytic Society which was attended by such luminaries as Sigmund Freud, Alfred Adler, Eduard Hitschmann, Otto Rank, and Wilhelm Stekel. Wittels raised three problems with regard to Kraus: the latter had become a journalist of his own inclination and then, when all paths to that goal had been smoothed out, "suddenly shifted gears, because of some personal motive, to become an 'anticorruptionist.' "[21] Later he changed again: "Journalists interest him no longer; he throws himself into the problem of sexuality."[22] Still later he became a writer of aphorisms, being contented with a "form of expression that is the most unimpassioned of all and is not suitable to permit so volcanic and high-spirited a writer to give full vent to his feelings."[23]

Wittels claims that Kraus's neurotic attitude toward one particular newspaper was the starting point of his hatred of journalists (Kraus's father was named Jacob, the "blessed one" of the Bible, "Benedictus" in the Vulgate, and Wittels sees significance in Kraus's attacks on men whose names start with a B: Benedikt—but, curiously enough, not Bacher, for some years the paper's codirector—Bahr, Bukowics, Bauer, and Buchbinder.) Wittels further claims that Kraus's relationships to his parents as well as to his siblings are filled with enmity:

He hates them, a circumstance that may perhaps explain a motive that was always recurring throughout his life: he attaches himself to someone in passionate friendship, which later turns into the bitterest enmity. . . . The continual repetition of this game in Kraus's life is the representation of the relationship of his brothers and himself to their father. . . . The capstone to this chain of evidence is the fact that the senior Kraus was a manufactuer and produced pulp for newspapers." [24]

In the second period of the *Fackel,* Wittels continues, Kraus's private neurosis became linked with the general neurosis of the time. "In this phase Kraus has, in some respects, himself lived through much of what Freud has found out by means of scientific work and has presented it in an artistic form." [25] But there was "an involution back into neurosis"; in fact, Wittels wished to demonstrate "how out of neurosis art emerges, and out of art once again neurosis." [26] "Kraus is a misshapen man," he goes on, "as was Voltaire, and as court jesters are described as having been. Mockery seems to be linked with physical deformity, and in that way to be suitable as a special domain of the Jews." [27]

In the discussion that followed Wittels' paper, Alfred Adler called Kraus "a philistine run wild, for whom the path to adequate self-indulgence became cut off;" [28] to Wilhelm Stekel, Kraus was "a paranoiac with a marked megalomania;" [29] and Dr. Friedjung delivered himself of the opinion that Kraus's "pedantic sense of form is perhaps to be derived from the fact that, in his parental home, German was not always spoken correctly and purely." [30] Sigmund Freud said that he could evaluate Kraus "only in a phenomenological and not in a moral sense"; [31] he had originally thought that in Kraus the cause of psychoanalysis could obtain an effective helper but had later recognized this to be an error in judgment: "He lacks any trace of self-mastery and seems to be altogether at the mercy of his instincts." [32] The minutes also record that "Freud personally finds Kraus's intellectual dependence on Peter Altenberg, who represents the estheticism of the impotent, distasteful." [33] On January 12, 1906, Freud had addressed a letter to Kraus in which he speaks of "the partial conformity between your views and endeavors and my own"[34] and disavows any complicity in the accusation of plagiarism leveled by Dr. Wilhelm Fliess against the late Otto Weininger and another writer. Freud is careful to point out, however, that he does not share Kraus's high regard for Weininger. Within the framework of Kraus's rejection of psycho-analysis, the evidence indicates that he respected Sigmund Freud personally—Krausian ideas are paralleled in *Civilization and Its Discontents* — but had little or no esteem for his disciples and imitators.

Before World War I, the publicist and critic Alfred Kerr edited a Berlin literary journal called *Pan.* Just as Maximilian Harden had tried to make capital out of his sensational revelations, Kerr trumped up the "affair" of the Berlin chief of police, Herr von Jagow, with the actress Tilla Durieux, who was married to Kerr's publisher Paul Cassirer. Kerr's titillating disclosures were published by the house of Cassirer, although its owner had thought the matter closed. In a series of articles on "Der Fall Kerr" ("The Kerr Case") published in the *Fackel* between March and July, 1911,[35] Kraus crossed quills with Kerr, whose style he saw as representing the death throes of feuilletonism. Declaring, in turn, that "Little Pan Is Dead," "Little Pan Still Emits a Death-Rattle," "Little Pan Stinks Already," "Little Pan Still Stinks," Kraus once again attempted to bring out the larger implications of what Kerr came to call *"fade Fehden"* (boring feuds). He wrote:

While other polemicists achieve popularity by running out of steam, the continued life of my objects keeps stimulating me. . . . I have often felt and said that the limits of polemics lie in the desire to use the inkwell instead of the pen. Luther, who knew how to write, brought himself to do so in his polemic against the devil.[36]

The Prague-born writer Max Brod came to Kerr's aid, declaring that "a mediocre mind like Karl Kraus, whose style only seldom avoids those two bad poles of literature, pathos and puns, should not be allowed to touch a poet, a creator, a pleasure-giver."[37] But Kraus claimed that no one in Germany could stand up to him, "even if they gird their loins with their admiration of Heine and the poet himself were resurrected on their side, for it is a fight with unequal weapons—the good cause versus the bad."[38] In July, 1911, Kerr published "Caprichos" in prose and poetry in *Pan.* Here, statements that Kraus is from the island of Microcephalonia and suffers from "double epigonnorhea"[39] (watered-down Spitzer and aped Harden) are followed by a scurrilously offensive lampoon of Kraus ("the strongest of my actions against Kerr thus far").[40] With this publication,

Kraus points out, Kerr has committed suicide. "It is my misfortune that the people whom I want to kill die as I lay hands on them. . . ." [41]

Yet there was life enough left in Kerr. During the war he published chauvinistic, bloodthirsty poems in a nationalistic newspaper, yet after the war he caused a small scandal by playing the role of an apostle of international brotherhood in Paris. Kraus reprinted some of the poems that had appeared under the pseudonym of "Gottlieb." As it turned out, "Gottlieb" had been the *nom de guerre* of several writers, and Kerr brought suit when Kraus falsely attributed one of these poems to him. During the litigation of 1927–28 a 208-page issue of *Fackel* was devoted to the subject "Der grösste Schuft im ganzen Land" ("The Greatest Scoundrel in the Whole Land"). [42] Kerr's supposedly last word in this unedifying affair, announced as a pamphlet to appear in September, 1928, never materialized. Kraus appears to have had the last word in 1930 when he demanded that Kerr give the money he had earned with his martial writings to disabled war veterans. The year before, Kraus had written apropos of "Kerrs Enthüllung" ("Kerr's Disclosure") that Bert Brecht was guilty of plagiarism by using an existing German translation of François Villon in his *Dreigroschenoper:* "In his little finger, with which he took some twenty-five verses of Ammer's translation of Villon, this fellow Brecht has more originality than that man Kerr who is stalking him." [43]

A Kraus disciple-turned-detractor was the Prague-born writer Willy Haas, originally an admirer who had helped organize Kraus's recitals in his native city. In 1913 he wrote: "I admire Kraus, for I regard him as pure and truthful"; [44] but in his autobiography, published in 1957, Haas called Kraus "a deliberate seducer and poisoner" and "a born sadist." [45] The "Correspondence With the *Literarische Welt*," the periodical edited by Haas (February–July, 1930) presumably had gone a long way toward changing Haas's mind. After denying Haas back copies of the *Fackel* which he had requested in connection with his study of Kraus's political views in changing times, Kraus remarks on the "rise of a Prague neophyte . . . to a *praeceptor Germaniae* in intellectual matters." [46] Haas's earlier attacks on Wilhelm Liebknecht, whom Kraus admired, and the practice of the *Literarischc Welt* of reviewing a book in the same issue in which it was advertised seem to have been sufficient grounds for Kraus to deny that periodical's raison d'être and break with Haas.

A noteworthy exception to this pattern is the writer Hans Müller who was a target of Kraus's satire in wartime. In his autobiography, the man later known, after his Swiss exile, as Hans Müller-Einigen says of

Kraus that "he bestowed upon me the distinction of his bitter enmity";
he speaks of Kraus's "pure, immaculate character" and calls him "an
offended, disappointed, betrayed dreamer. . . . His collected works . . .
belong among the imperishably sparse works of compassionate
love." [47] A wholly gratifying phenomenon was the artist Albert Bloch,
Kraus's tireless propagator in the United States and thus far his only
"official" translator into English. Bloch, born in 1882 in St. Louis,
went to Europe in 1908 and lived in Munich for a dozen years. From
1911 until the outbreak of the war he was associated with Franz Marc
and Wassily Kandinsky in the *Blaue Reiter* group, and his interest in
Kraus dates from that period. In 1921 Bloch returned to the United
States, and from 1923 until his retirement he headed the Department
of Painting and Drawing at the University of Kansas. He died in 1961.
The *Fackel* of March, 1925, carries a letter from Bloch in which he
states that his native English benefited from the German he read in that
periodical.[48] On the occasion of Kraus's birthday in 1928, Bloch
lyrically expressed his indebtedness to Kraus.

> Master to whom I owe my mind's rebirth,
> teacher, whose precept makes to shine more clear
> the truths at which with purblind eyes the earth
> blinks unbelieving or with cynic leer;
> O judge and prophet, whose decree austere
> lashes unscathed the thick hide of unworth;
> You poet martyr, whose own tortured jeer
> looses the mob's misunderstanding mirth—
>
> Accept, now that the leaves of life grow wan,
> this birthday wish of one you've never met.
> May Springtide dwell within, though Fall come on,
> And may your sun still rise, what though it set.
> Bright leap the flame within my spirit's house,
> by your word kindled, well-beloved Karl Kraus . . .[49]

In his Foreword to his edition of Kraus's *Poems*, which includes
excerpts from *Die letzten Tage der Menschheit* (at Kraus's request,
Theodor Haecker had testified to the quality of the translation), Bloch
calls Kraus the "greatest writer of German verse and prose since
Goethe" and "the most ardent ethical force at work in the world
today." [50]

III *Another Literature Demolished*

The Prague-born poet, novelist, and dramatist Franz Werfel, one of
the leading figures among the early literary Expressionists, was a

youthful admirer of Kraus, who, in turn, had printed and recited several of Werfel's poems and announced his early collections in the *Fackel*. In 1912 Werfel went to Leipzig to become an editor in the house of Kurt Wolff, who was to become one of the great publishers of his time and is particularly noted for his early championship of German Expressionism. Werfel shared his immense enthusiasm for Kraus with his new employer and advised him to become Kraus's publisher. Wolff went to Vienna and spent many stimulating hours with Kraus, who told him about his plans for a volume to be entitled *Kultur und Presse*. It never appeared, but in 1914 Wolff did publish a de luxe edition of the essay "Die chinesische Mauer" with monumental lithographs by Oskar Kokoschka.

Since Kraus balked at the idea of sharing a publisher with writers he disapproved of, Wolff founded a separate firm known as Verlag der Schriften von Karl Kraus (Kurt Wolff). Between 1916 and 1920 this house published five volumes of Kraus's poetry and three volumes of essays, in addition to reprinting several of the earlier works that had been brought out by other publishers—fourteen titles in all. But Franz Werfel, the man who had contributed a dithyrambic essay to Ludwig von Ficker's *Rundfrage über Karl Kraus*, in which he described his encounter with Kraus as "a mystical experience" and spoke of "the hour which binds my planet to his" [51], had turned away from Kraus even before his essay appeared in pamphlet form. In the *Fackel* of November, 1916, Kraus had published a poem entitled "Elysisches: Melancholie an Kurt Wolff"; [52] in the form of a complaint to Wolff, this is a subtle stylistic persiflage of the Goethean-Schillerian pathos and the posturings and lyrical feuilletonism of Werfel and other Jewish writers from Prague with neo-Catholic pretensions. Werfel's impetuous letter of protest, in which he questioned Kraus's poetic talent and chided him for using the word *"dorten"* (which, far from being merely German-Jewish jargon, has been used by eminent poets), elicited a devastating satirical gloss with that title. [53]

Werfel's reply was "Metaphysik des Drehs" ("The Metaphysics of the Dodge"), an open letter full of invective like "egomaniacal suicidal type"; it was published in *Die Aktion* and reprinted in the *Fackel* for October, 1918. [54] In a retaliatory essay, "Aus der Sudelküche" ("From the Slovenly Kitchen"), [55] Kraus lampooned Werfel for his pathos-filled stance of cosmic empathy with all mankind. Werfel thereupon shifted the battle to the field of literature. His poem "Einem Denker" ("To a Thinker"), which appears in Werfel's 1919 collection *Gerichtstag*

(Judgment Day), reflects his new view of Kraus as a crafty and self-righteous judge. In the third part of Werfel's "Magical Trilogy" *Spiegelmensch (Mirror Man)*, the title character delivers a vulgar prose soliloquy. (Kurt Wolff's unsuccessful attempt to delete it from the book edition of the play, which appeared under his imprint in 1920, meant that, from the following year on, Kraus's writings appeared in the Verlag *"Die Fackel,"* Vienna, which was identical with the firm of Jahoda & Siegel).

What shall I do in the coming days of idleness? I've got it! I will join the prophets—the major prophets, of course. To begin with, I shall found . . . a periodical and call it—The Lamp? No! The Candle Stump? No! The Torch? Yes! Ah! My fingers are itching with all the great writers of world literature! People shall think that Goethe plus Shakespeare's genius has been reincarnated in the form of a shyster lawyer from the East. I will turn city gossip into a cosmic event and cosmic events into city gossip. I will juggle puns and pathos so skillfully that everyone who feels, after reading the first line, that I am a comical informer and fartcatcher [*Fürzefänger*] will have to admit, upon reading the next line, that I am Isaiah incarnate. But, above all, I will appear as the cabaret performer of my apocalyptic preachings, for I am a good comedian, and that is what I am recognized by, to say nothing of my ability as an imitator of voices and . . . an acoustic mirror.[56]

Kraus struck back promptly—with a "Magical Operetta in Two Parts" entitled *Literatur oder Man wird doch da sehn (Literature or We Shall See About That)*. He first read it in Vienna on March 6, 1921, a month before *Spiegelmensch* had its premiere at the Burgtheater. The printed program contains pertinent passages from *Spiegelmensch* (as does the book edition of the same year) as well as this notice: "For an understanding of the action, familiarity with *Spiegelmensch* is indispensable; with *Faust*, desirable."

For the second time Kraus demolishes a literature (Expressionism rather than Young Vienna)—this time not with witty glosses and *aperçus* but by letting it manifest its unworth and speak its death warrant directly. Again the scene is a café—the Central rather than the Griensteidl—and the Werfel figure is named Johann Wolfgang. His father reproaches him for not having entered his business: "Instead of writing books, you people ought to be keeping them." [57] The father has heard that his son's poetry is unoriginal and derivative, reminiscent of an old classic named Werfel; yet even he is inspired to speak poetically and epigrammatically when he sees his son. In true Expressionistic fashion, the pompous son rebels against his father; the Mirror Man's statement "The heritage that you can't escape–kill it in order to possess it" [58] is an adaptation of both the Goethean "What you have inherited from your fathers, earn it [*erwirb es*] so as to possess it" and the Expressionists' variant "What you have inherited from your fathers, reject it [*verwirf es*] in order to possess yourself."

The son's cousin Johann Paul recites his typical Expressionist poem in telescoped eruptive style; he is Georg Kulka, the young writer who had fooled the Burgtheater by getting it to print, in one of its program booklets, an essay by Jean Paul under his own name–supposedly to promote a favorite, and neglected, author. (Kraus's exposure of Kulka had induced Albert Ehrenstein, a once-honored member of the *Fackel* family, to assert in a pamphlet that "Saint Crausiscus of Narcissi" [59] had, in his poem "Apokalypse," [60] plagiarized the New Testament). Other topical references are to Werfel's revolutionary speech in postwar Vienna exhorting the people to storm the Bankverein, and to literary figures like Fritz von Unruh, Hugo Sonnenschein, Stefan Zweig, and Hermann Bahr.

The bourgeois bacchantes and meandering maenads in the café produce a flavorful brew of journalistic jargon, coffee-house commerce, and Expressionistic ecstasy. The play is replete with lines from *Faust* or adaptations thereof, whereas Johann Paul's soliloquy is full of Werfelian allusions. The characters named Harald Brüller and Brahmanuel Leiser represent two then-current *Weltanschauungen.* (H. H. Hahnl has pointed out that the source for both was Robert Müller, a writer who had published an unfriendly pamphlet on Kraus in 1914 and had also put Kraus in his play *Die Politiker des Geistes* [1917] as Ekkehard Meyer, the editor of *Geist.* Leiser is supposed to be a "Bolshevik and a gentleman";[61] and this is the title of a collection of essays by Müller which appeared in 1920.) [62] In a conversation between two maenads that is full of pseudo-religious vaporings, Kraus satirizes the effect which Expressionists, fashionable pseudo-philosophical essayists, psychoanalysts, and other "redeemers" have had on the impressionable *hoi polloi.* One maenad compares *Spiegelmensch* with *Faust,* to the detriment of the latter.

In Part Two, one literary bacchant is unsure as to whether to join neo-Catholicism or Zionism. Kraus has, of course, put himself into the play again, and the father repeats all the familiar gossip and imputations of base motives current about him for years. There is a general chorus of "That's his father complex . . . Jewish self-hatred . . . All he knows is how to imitate our Jewish accent . . . epigone . . . we have material

against him ... I'm working on a novel that attacks him ... The play
I'm working on will finish him off; the publisher's blurb is
ready ...."[63] The son refers to Kraus by the Mephistophelian epithet,
"the spirit that always negates."[64] Enter Schwarz-Drucker (Ink-
printer), an operetta Benedikt, along with his friend Frei-Handl
(Freetrade), and offers the people his (i.e., the *Neue Freie Presse*'s)
services if they want to fight Kraus. "Who does not know today that a
single day of our activity has influenced intellectual life more decisively
than the collected works of Goethe? ... Do you want fame? The press
will give it to you. Do you want a career? The press will give you
one.... There is nothing the press won't *bringen*" (bring/print).[65]
Schwarz-Drucker launches into a chanson, a concentrated account of
Creation, which became a Kraus favorite.

The Press

Before we started printing
there was no heaven or earth.
For these are of our minting,
to us they owe their birth.
They issued from our vapor
—God saw, and took the hint—
and so the world as paper
we print.

The world was well contented,
rotating by our grace;
for have we not consented
to give it time and space?
Events, too, that occurred not
we play up without sting;
it's news and so, deterred not,
we print!

What though the sheet be lousy
our readers always bite;
our lies, however frowsy,
are truth: they're black on white.
However we deceive it
and by whatever dint,
the world must needs believe it
in print.

They read what we've selected
they think what we suggest.
Still greater gain's expected
from news that is suppressed.
We're silent or we scribble,
at call we change our tint,
while greedily they nibble
our print.

The world of faithful readers
sings loud our melody.
We still remain its leaders—
thank God the press is free.
In time to our mad measure
men dance and limp and sprint,
as thanks for their sad pleasure
in print.

This age for reading hungers,
it eats it from our hand,
for we are culture-mongers,
well-known in every land.
Come on, you scholars, thinkers,
you, who with envy squint
at smart, well-paid hoodwinkers—
come, print!

So printing, hinting, minting,
we make life what we will.
True worth endures no tinting,
delusion brings the thrill.
Black as the regions hellish
and yellow as sulphur's glint,
the devil's imps embellish
news-print! [66]

When the son throws a coffee cup at his father, a Mirror Man appears and shields the latter; the man is Kraus, and he finally disintegrates. Publisher's Blurb appears and stuns everyone with the extravagance of his rhapsodic statements: "This Magic Trilogy is a drama suckled on Calderonian mysticism, Molièrian comedy, Aristophanean boldness, and Werfelian depth. . . ." [67] Having come to the conclusion that "only art is good business today" [68], the father makes up with his reborn and purified son. Not only have we witnessed the marriage of business and literature, but the writer Franz Blei, appearing in an abbot's garb, cries "Long live Communism and the Catholic Church." [69] Although Kraus

has concentrated his parody on the father-son motive in *Spiegelmensch,*
he follows Werfel's drama in a number of other places, including the
end, where Werfel has an abbot appear. Werfel's "26 Mönche" ("26
Monks") have turned into Kraus's "26 Schmöcke" ("26 Prigs").[70]

Literatur is an operetta by virtue of an overture, the opening chorus
of bacchants, entr'acte music, the songs of the two maenads and of
Chloe Goldenberg, and Schwarz-Drucker's chanson. The music, included with the book edition, is "according to the specifications of the
author." Max Brod complained that "Kraus acknowledged the hospi-
tality graciously accorded him by Werfel's family by sketching a
distorted, shameful portrait of Werfel's father—one that was . . . utterly
inappropriate. . . . Not one feature of the caricature is correct." [71]
Brod also reports that *Literatur* inspired his friend Franz Kafka to agree
with some of Kraus's observations on Jewish writers in the German
language. A remark made by Kafka to Brod is as perceptive as it is
pertinent: "In the hell of German-Jewish letters Kraus is the great
overseer and taskmaster . . . but he forgets that he himself belongs in
this hell among those to be chastised." [72]

The feud between Kraus and Werfel was renewed in Werfel's play
Paul Among the Jews (1926), in which Paul, an advocate of Christian
love, prevails over the cold and heartless Rabbi Beschwörer, a Kraus
figure, who has hitherto held sway via the vanity of the word; in
Werfel's poem of the following year, "Der Fanatiker"; in a scene in
Kraus's play *Wolkenkuckucksheim;* and in several glosses in the *Fackel.*
But Kurt Wolff reports a poignant and rather revealing statement made
by Werfel to a mutual friend in his last years: "If Kraus had lived long
enough to be forced to emigrate, as I was, I would have gone to him
and made my peace with him." [73]

IV Die Unüberwindlichen

In the middle and late 1920s, Kraus castigated the unholy alliance
between a police chief who, with bureaucratic *Gemütlichkeit,* retouched the record of a corrupt newspaper czar, and a press boss who
ordered his editors to print nothing about ninety dead persons on the
police chief's conscience.

Imre (Emmerich) Békessy had arrived in Vienna from his native
Budapest in 1920, at the age of thirty-three. He rapidly gained strong
influence in Vienna's public life by founding four newspapers and
journals, a press empire shored up by great sums of money and a coterie
of sycophants: *Die Stunde,* a daily founded in 1923, the year in which

Békessy acquired Austrian citizenship; *Die Bühne,* an illustrated weekly; *Die Börse,* a financial journal; and *Die Sphinx,* which was devoted to the interpretation of dreams and to crossword puzzles. By 1924 Békessy was the uncrowned newspaper king of Vienna and the leader in the postwar dance around the Golden Calf.

Kraus began his fight against the man whom he called the "Buda pest" early in 1925; for him Békessy was simply a collective name for the putrefaction of the postwar period. To his articles, several of which were read in public, *Die Stunde*–a "modern" paper which tried to revamp all moral values–reacted by having Békessy's minions Anton Kuh and Felix Salten attack Kraus; the former delivered a scurrilous and stormy impromptu speech on Kraus, "Der Affe Zarathustras" ("Zarathustra's Ape"), in a Vienna auditorium on October 25, 1925. During the three-year Békessiad, the newspaper czar and extortioner brought suit against two men who had exposed him, Gustav Stolper and Karl Federn, the editors of *Der österreichische Volkswirt,* an economic journal, and missed no opportunity to denigrate Kraus (e.g., by printing retouched photos which made him look like an imbecile). On June 25, 1925, Kraus cried "Hinaus aus Wien mit dem Schuft!" (Kick the crook out of Vienna!) before nine hundred people in the Mittlerer Konzerthaussaal. This ringing slogan became the leitmotif of his polemic[74] and soon reverberated throughout Vienna, although people were too slothful or too afraid to act. A courageous public prosecutor having brought two of Békessy's cohorts to bay, a warrant was finally issued for Békessy's arrest. Békessy fled from Vienna in the summer of 1926–first to Paris and then to Budapest.

On January 30, 1927, there was a clash between two paramilitary organizations, the republican Schutzbund and the rightist Heimwehr, at Schattendorf, a small border town in the Burgenland province. The Heimwehr, as the aggressor, inflicted two casualties on the Schutzbund. On July 14, the killers were acquitted by a Vienna jury, a verdict that aroused much popular indignation. On the following day, a spontaneous demonstration took place on the Ringstrasse. Unknown arsonists broke into the Justizpalast, the Ministry of Justice, and set documents on fire; the crowd denied access to the fire brigade even though Mayor Karl Seitz appeared at its head. Under their chief Johann(es) Schober the police rioted and haphazardly fired into the crowd with Dum Dum bullets, causing ninety deaths and some three hundred injuries. Foreign correspondents gave the lie to the official police version that they had acted in self-defense against an organized demonstration. Even though as early as 1926 Schober had promised Kraus to help him against Békessy, it turned out that he had been shielding the press czar by suppressing the ample evidence that existed against him. Kraus now took on the police chief as well; in him he recognized a type familiar from the world war: the jovial executioner. In September, 1927, he had posters with the following text affixed throughout Vienna:

> To Johann Schober, Police Chief of Vienna.
> I demand that you resign.
> Karl Kraus
> Editor of the *Fackel*

(The effectiveness of this bold move was, to be sure, somewhat diminished, that is, shifted to the areas of self-advertisement and comedy, by a counterposter put up by a "character" named Ernst Winkler, known as the "Goldfüllfederkönig" [Gold Fountain Pen King].

> To Johann Schober, Police Chief of Vienna.
> *I* demand that you do *not* resign.
> Gold Fountain Pen King
> E.W.)

Once more Kraus was dealing with "a reality which catches up with satire every hour." [75] The *Fackel* for October, 1927 was devoted to his fight against Schober.

Die Unüberwindlichen (The Unconquerable), Kraus's "Postwar Play in Four Acts," was written between December, 1927, and February, 1928, has as its motto the Kierkegaardian aphorism which heads this chapter, and is dedicated to Oskar Samek, Kraus's friend and trusted attorney, whose services were especially valuable in the Békessy-Schober affair. [76] The play combines a Békessiad with a Schoberiad. "Once again, as in the last days of a mankind whose mysterious continued existence has now given us these scenes," wrote Kraus in his Preface, "documents have become figures, reports have materialized as forms, and clichés stand on two legs." [77]

Act One of the play is subtitled "Those of *Die Pfeife*" (The Whistle). Barkassy is the publisher (*"Barkasse"* means "cash money") and Fallotai the editorial secretary (*"Fallot,"* "rascal," with a Hungarian ending) of this scandal sheet which, to use a pertinent pun made in a different context by Theodor Herzl, seems to be "auf der Erpresse gedruckt" (sent through the blackmail). Barkassy is bothered by echoes of "Hinaus aus Wien mit dem Schuft!", but Fallotai reassures him: "One fanatic isn't going to change the world, and the world has accepted us. . . . We are here! More than that: the world is becoming like us. . . . Our strength is every weakness there is. . . . Our program is to have none. . . . Live and let live—that is the idea you have taught the Viennese again." [78] Both give a list of the "bread and circuses" they have given Vienna. Fallotai reminds Barkassy that he fired an editor because he once wrote the truth—" though only in an inconspicuous place where no one would have noticed it." [79] "One doesn't tell the truth unnecessarily," says Barkassy, "nor does one tell lies indiscriminately. . . . Everything must be nicely distributed so the readers can't tell; they should see spots in front of their eyes . . . I tickle Achilles heels." [80]

Act Two, "Die Diesbezüglichen" ("The With Respect to This-ers"), introduces the police chief, here named Wacker (Doughty), and his two flunkeys named—after Schober's convoluted officialese—Hinsichtl and Rücksichtl (Concernin and Considerin). The character named Veilchen (Violet), of the "negroid type," is the real-life Hofrat Bernhard Pollak, head of the political police. He is given to using French and Latin clichés, so that his speeches are often almost macaronic; he keeps saying the same thing, and grandiloquent phrases are used trivially to comic effect. Using the split-stage technique, Kraus has the scenes in this act alternate. While the editor of *Der Pfeil (The Arrow)*, Arkus (an anagram of Kraus's name), calls on the chief, Hofrat Veilchen and Barkassy converse next door. "Your success as a stimulator of Viennese life is incontestable" [81], says the Hofrat, whom Barkassy has asked to help him out of a scrape. "The Vienna police is the last authority that I'd permit to spoil my business," says Barkassy. "I am truth! Don't you make the times better than they are. I am their expression!" [82] Meanwhile Arkus has given Wacker incriminating documents dated Budapest, 1923, and showing that sixteen proceedings are pending against Barkassy; yet everyone is afraid of moving against the blackmailer who had engaged in nefarious activities during the war as well. While Wacker and Veilchen exchange notes, the chief receives a call from his superior Vollmann (Kollmann, the Christian Socialist Finance Minister): everything is all right, and Barkassy's *Leumundsnote* (record) will be cleaned up.

Act Three, "Paris Life," takes us to the boudoir of Baron Camillioni (Camillo Castiglioni, the shady financeer and profiteer of the inflationary period) who has heard that Barkassy is on his way to Paris. "Typically Austrian . . . Fascism tempered by sloppiness." [83] He has heard about the poster which *Pfeil*-Arkus has put up "by way of giving himself publicity . . . He got him out—but he won't get me in!" [84] Barkassy calls on Camillioni and tells him that he has tried to commit suicide. (Békessy made numerous attempts from 1926 on, finally succeeding in Budapest in 1951.) [85] The two self-styled "Renaissance criminals" commiserate with each other. Camillioni: "Yesterday *per du* [on familiar terms] with those in power. . . ." Barkassy: ". . . today *perdu* [lost].[86] Yet Barkassy is determined to make a comeback in Vienna. When he says that he is going to rise Phoenix-like, Camillioni reminds him that Phoenix is the name of a Vienna burglary insurance company. But he concedes that with all he knows about the private lives of Vienna's public figures, Barkassy should really be the chief of police. As one crook to another (a third, the banker Sigmund Bosel, is mentioned in the play as Lobes), Camillioni says that Barkassy has cost him eight million so far. Barkassy: "I've come to ask you for the ninth." [87]

The final act, "Silent Night, Holy Night," takes place after the Justizpalast fire and police massacre. (In the Preface Kraus admits that what he depicts in the final act has not taken place at the time of writing. But reality will probably soon catch up with his vision, "for the bourgeois world of decay and chance needs a blackmailer as a scourge in a state of degeneracy where all revolutionary threats have lost their terror.") [88] At the Vienna police headquarters, a Christmas celebration in honor of the chief is in progress. Wacker sings the "Schoberlied" with its endless rhymes on "Pflicht" (duty): "Can't you see that it's my duty . . . not to resign from office? . . . But it's not my duty to appear in court." [89] Sung to a tune combining elements of the Radetzky March with the old song "Üb' immer Treu' und Redlichkeit" (which, in turn, uses the melody of Mozart's "Ein Mädchen oder Weibchen" from *The Magic Flute*), it became a Kraus favorite.[90]

When the marionette-like Hinsichtl and Rücksichtl once inadvertently speak the truth ("They shot almost exclusively at defenseless, fleeing people"),[91] Veilchen thinks that something is wrong with them and examines their mechanism. A Prominent Dutchman has come to speak favorably of the behavior of the police on July 15 and 16. Making long, chiché-ridden speeches, Wacker says that there were only 90 dead, 32 of them with criminal records; the same is true of 74 of the 281 injured civilians; the child victims have not been checked out as yet. Hinsicht and Rücksichtl each step forward and tell it "like it was": Even people trying to remove the dead were shot at by the police . . . shots were fired into a theater and into city hall . . . any gathering of people was shot at . . . pregnant women were trampled to death . . . even first-aid vehicles were fired at . . . doctors were beaten, firemen attacked, children shot. And after such a bloodbath the police are given votes of confidence! "Those days in Vienna were proof that the police of the Austrian capital is one of the most medieval institutions." [92]

Like a dual dybbuk, these two seem to be the voices of many, including witnesses beaten and cowed by policemen in their *Watschenmaschine* (slapping machine). But Wacker speaks the magic words *"Treue um Treue"* [93] (loyalty for loyalty), and the two revert to being obedient functionaries. Wacker attributes their later lapses to overwork and the poisonous enemy documents which his staff has had to read. A character named Ramatamer (a bit of Viennese dialect meaning something like "Cleanemup") who has hitherto been kept in check now breaks loose and gives a drunken monologue about his exploits. Veilchen reads a telegram announcing Barkassy's return. Presently the exile appears, ready to forgive, forget, and start a *Neue Pfeife*. He feels the strength of an Antaeus now that he has Viennese soil under his feet again. "What, you banish the man who has reached the hearts of the Viennese like no other man . . . I handled the after-treatment of the so-called revolution, but I was interrupted . . . I had to come back, because you need me. Your society can't live without me. You are getting too cocky." [94] Barkassy magnanimously forgives Wacker and asks him what steps he intends to take against Arkus. They agree to give him the silent treatment. "Today I realize," says Barkassy, "that the aristocratic tactic of the *Neue Freie Presse* was the only correct one. . . . We can both say that we have hurt him more deeply in his vanity than his satire was ever able to hurt us." [95] Wacker has heard that Arkus is writing a play dealing with what seems to be the diametrically opposed worlds of the two, but, as Barkassy points out, they really are closely connected. The play comes to a tragicomic end under the Christmas tree, with Barkassy wondering whether one can dance the Charleston to "Silent Night, Holy Night."

Kraus gave readings of his play in Vienna, Prague, and Berlin in May, 1928. Following a performance at a Dresden actors' studio in May, 1929, the official premiere of *Die Unüberwindlichen* took place in Berlin on October 20, 1929, with a stellar cast: Peter Lorre as Barkassy,

Ernst Ginsberg as Arkus, Hans Peppler as Wacker, Leonhard Steckel as Veilchen, and Kurt Gerron as Camillioni. The cartoonist B. F. Dolbin designed the sets and created the makeup. *Der Stürmer* reviewed this performance and regarded the play as a panegyric on the Jewish race in opposition to Germans because the "heroes" were Jews. Further performances were canceled at the behest of the Austrian Embassy. In November and December, 1931, the play was performed in Leipzig. *Die Unüberwindlichen* is a *pièce à clef,* a sort of dramatized special issue of the *Fackel,* and it demonstrates that plays of standard length were not Kraus's forte. However, in the light of the later development of the German-language theater, this play, with its use of recent historical events and real-life characters, foreshadows the documentary plays which have held the German stage in recent years. If *Die letzten Tage der Menschheit* may be said to have influenced both the technique and the substance of Brecht's *Furcht und Elend des Dritten Reiches (The Private Life of the Master Race), Die Unüberwindlichen* foreshadows the same playwright's *Der aufhaltsame Aufstieg des Arturo Ui (The Resistible Rise of Arturo Ui)* as well as Sartre's *Nekrassov.*

Békessy did not return to Vienna, and when one considers that Kraus here prevailed against a clique and a claque, that he did single-handedly "kick the crook out of Vienna," it is tempting to assume that for once the Great Boyg was successfully hit. Yet the climate for crookedness remained; Chancellor Seipel called Johannes Schober "the shield of the Republic"; Schober became the Chancellor of Austria in September, 1929, serving for one year; and it continued to be painfully evident to Kraus that his admirers turned detractors and the combined forces of the press, the financiers, and the police in the first Austrian Republic were truly unconquerable.

CHAPTER 7

The "Theater of Poetry"

I "Performer: Karl Kraus"

KARL KRAUS'S recitals of his own works and those of others were not a random extension of his sphere of influence, the way a successful author or scholar may undertake public addresses or lecture tours, but must be regarded as an integral part of his creativity—indeed, as the very apogee of his effectiveness. On these frequent and memorable occasions Kraus served language by giving the spoken word its due. With his "Theater of Poetry" he institutionalized his love of the theater and protested against the superficiality of the commercial theater. For many years his literary evenings were announced simply as "Vorlesung Karl Kraus" ("Recital by Karl Kraus"); from 1925 on Kraus used "Theater der Dichtung" as a subheading, and in the last few years of his life the programs were announced as "Theater der Dichtung. Darsteller: Karl Kraus" ("Theater of Poetry. Performer: Karl Kraus"). There is much justification for designating *all* of Kraus's recitals as "Theater of Poetry"; it should be borne in mind, however, that *"Dichtung"* means not just lyric poetry, but creative writing in general. Kraus said of himself that he was perhaps the first writer to experience his writing as an actor. "When I read, it is not acted literature," he wrote; "but what I write is written acting." [1] A more general statement of his purpose runs as follows: "By way of motivating a literary evening: It is literature when something thought is at the same time something seen and heard." [2]

Kraus's first *Vorlesung* was private and took place in Vienna on October 21, 1892. It was entitled "Im Reiche der Kothpoeten oder Zwei Stunden modern" ("In the Realm of the Muck Poets [this is what Ludwig Speidel had called the Naturalists] or Two Hours of Modern Literature"). On that occasion, Kraus read from the works of Liliencron, Bierbaum, Holz, Busse, and others. This was followed by a reading at Ischl of Gerhart Hauptmann's drama *Die Weber (The Weavers)* in August of the same year; it was so successful that Kraus repeated it in Munich and Vienna. Yet, somewhat surprisingly, there ensued a big hiatus in this activity, and Kraus did not resume his recitals until January, 1910, when he read from his own works in Berlin. At his first public evening in Vienna on May 3 of that year he read *Heine und die Folgen* before such a packed house that he had to repeat the recital a month later. In December, 1910, Kraus undertook his first lecture tour. He gave seven hundred public readings in all, the last one taking place in Vienna on April 2, 1936, before an invited audience. Of these recitals, 414 took place in Vienna, 105 in Berlin, 57 in Prague, 17 in Munich, and 10 in Paris; the others were given in various German, Austrian, Swiss, Czech, Hungarian, and Italian cities. The three hundredth recital coincided with the twenty-fifth anniversary of *Die Fackel* in 1924, and the five hundredth reading celebrated its thirtieth anniversary. Kraus, who had an eye for such statistics, said that he read his own writings on 260 occasions and those of others on 302; 138 were "mixed."

In the "Theater of Poetry," Kraus wanted to demonstrate his creative process to others, to give them an insight into the creative tension, the purging passion, and the cathartic quality that informed his work. His reading of his works was a re-creactive act—re-creation and education rather than recreation or entertainment. These evenings undoubtedly were a necessary therapy for him and great psychological satisfaction. His attitude toward his audiences is expressed in an epigram entitled "Der Vorleser" [3] ("The Reciter"): he does not recognize them as individuals but must unite them into an audience, turn them into a feeling, reacting mass. Praise or blame has nothing to do with his effectiveness; let people censure him in the cloakroom, but in the lecture hall they were all defenseless.

"The atmosphere of such a recital is full of taut energy," wrote Leopold Liegler, "because it is always a matter of one against all and because this one man calls the world before his judge's bench in enormous public legal proceedings. Through the force of his pathos the listeners are removed from their petty selves and lifted to a height of experience which they would never have attained on their own." [4] Kraus sought to achieve his effects with a remarkable economy of means. He felt that it was the foremost task of the theater to stir the human imagination; consequently he was opposed to all external effects, such as the opulence of Max Reinhardt's productions and the technical devices of Erwin Piscator, which tended to overwhelm the words of a poet. Kraus proudly dispensed with the customary trappings of lectures

and other one-man theaters, spurning even the customary glass of water
by the lectern. He never recited from memory: "Not memory but
presence of mind is the element that is drawn from on the podium." [5]
His voice, which could fill the largest halls, was capable of a
well-modulated lyrical quality as well as vociferous dramatic outbursts.
In its musicality, vibrancy, and striking expressiveness it was somewhat
reminiscent of that of the actor Alexander Moissi (whom Kraus did *not*
admire). Erich Heller has emphasized Kraus's directness of communication:

What his spellbound audiences witnessed was not an impersonation of
different characters. He neither moved about the stage nor changed his
voice in the manner of the ventriloquist. Yet the scene was alive with a
multitude of voices, and full of genuine dramatic tension. It was as
though the gulf had been bridged between the dramatic imagination of
the poet and the inevitable inadequacies of the "real life" of his figures
on a real stage. Karl Kraus took his listeners to the very center of poetic
creation. . . . His theater bestowed upon dramatic poetry the privilege
which any competently performed piece of music enjoys: the directness
of communication, the freedom from interference by the unwieldiness
of matter.[6]

The Danish writer Karin Michaelis has furnished a valuable account of a
Kraus recital in 1911.

All the lights have been extinguished. Only two candles shed their light
up there on the green-covered table. They sparkle uncannily. Now
comes Kraus. Young, with long, uncontrolled limbs, shy as a bat, he
hurries to the table, anxiously barricades himself behind it, crosses his
legs, strokes his forehead, wipes his nose, collects himself like a beast of
prey ready to leap, waits, opens his mouth as if to bite, shuts it again,
waits.
    An infinitely gentle, infinitely sad smile trembles over his face. A
fleeting, stately, shy joy melts all severity in his young, intelligent,
embittered-looking face. His nervous hands move over the manuscripts
which he has brought along. He begins—sternly, thoughtfully, ener-
getically, compellingly, compelling through conviction. If he had
spoken in Chinese or Persian, people would have followed him with
equal suspense. His own inner fire has the same effect as the spark from
a locomotive rushing by on a summer-parched prairie: everything flares
up while he speaks. For an hour and a quarter he brandishes the blade
of the word. Now his voice is hoarse with quiet rage, now it sounds
melodious, as if he were inserting a stanza from a folk song; now it rises
to a roaring storm in which one can hardly distinguish a word from a
scream, at another moment it pierces the air like blows from gleaming

weapons. ... He pauses and hurries outside. He hurries, flees—his shadow appears in huge outline on the black wall—and disappears behind a curtain.[7]

After hearing Kraus read in Innsbruck in 1911, the Austrian poet Georg Trakl apostrophized him as the

> White high priest of truth.
> Crystal voice in which God's icy breath dwells.
> Angry magician
> Under whose black cloak clangs the blue armor
>   of the warrior.[8]

Kraus's most anxious moment at these recitals came between the green room and the green table; suddenly he felt exposed as a *Privatperson;* only after the first word had been spoken was he in his element. Instead of bowing to applause, Kraus customarily acknowledged it by reappearing and peering intently at his audience.

Kraus bestowed as much care on a recital as he did on an issue of the *Fackel* or one of his books. The printed programs for these evenings— collector's items today—are meticulous little works of scholarship, often including information about the circumstances of first performances or printings as well as the history and relevance of a work. Walter Benjamin has pointed out that the "barbed wire" [9] of editorial announcements fencing in each issue of the *Fackel* as well as the razor-sharp definitions in the programs of Kraus's public readings were really defense mechanisms. It is not surprising that even though Kraus's recitals were enjoyed by many thousands, not a word about them appeared in the Austrian press; announcements in the *Fackel* and on posters generally sufficed to bring in capacity audiences. Because the press was feared in the early years, certain Viennese halls, such as the acoustically perfect Bösendorfersaal and the auditorium of the Urania, were not available to Kraus, but the great success of these evenings eventually opened all halls to him.

From the beginning of the war until the end of Kraus's life, the proceeds from these readings were given to charity, usually those causes that were neglected by self-seeking do-gooders. Kraus benefited ill or indigent poets like Peter Altenberg (he started a fund for his gravestone) and Else Lasker-Schüler, Children's Aid, the blind and the starving at home and abroad, unemployed youths, and the Friends' Relief Mission; in one case, part of the proceeds went "to a 15-year-old boy who recently made a vain attempt to keep his unemployed father from committing suicide."[10] Moneys won by Kraus in suits for plagiarism and reprint fees went to such charities as well.

Kraus regularly read from the works of Gerhart Hauptmann (*Die Weber* and *Hanneles Himmelfahrt* [*The Ascension of Hannele*] rather than the later dramas), Bert Brecht, Peter Altenberg, Frank Wedekind, Goethe (*Pandora;* Act III of *Faust,* Part Two), Liliencron, Gogol *(Der Revisor),* Strindberg, and Raimund *(Der Verschwender* [*The Spendthrift*]). His readings of works by half-forgotten German poets of the seventeenth and eighteenth centuries from Gryphius to Matthias Claudius (Paul Fleming, Johann Klaj, J. C. Günther, J. E. Schlegel, Hölty, Göckingh) inspired several anthologies of these poets.[11] In February, 1920, two recitals were scheduled for Innsbruck; the second one had to be canceled by the police because Pan-German students, incited by the press, had threatened to disrupt the evening.

In the early 1920s Kraus's readings were given before ever increasing audiences of workers; however, the *Kulturstelle* (cultural department) of the Social Democratic party soon enough resented Kraus's criticism of its policies and did its utmost to isolate this unwelcome gadfly. Between 1925 and 1927 Kraus also gave recitals in Paris, reading mostly from his antiwar writings. (In 1925 nine French university professors, including Charles Andler, Ferdinand Brunot, and Lucien Levy-Bruhl, nominated him for the 1926 Nobel Prize for Literature; the proposal was renewed twice).[12] On December 14, 1930, Kraus read *A Winter's Tale* for three hundred Viennese high school students at their own request. In January, 1932, he gave a program of poems and scenes by Bert Brecht, accompanied on the piano by Kurt Weill.

Many of Kraus's literary and dramatic programs included songs and musical interludes; his piano accompanists from 1914 on were Georg Knepler, Viktor Junk, Franz Mittler, Josef Bartosch, Karl Meyer, Otto Janowitz, Bruno Hartig, Jan Sliwinski, Friedrich Hollaender, Karol Rathaus, Eugen Auerbach, and Herbert Breth Mildner. Franz Mittler, Ernst Křenek, Mechtilde Lichnowsky, Josef Matthias Hauer, Dora Pejacsevich, and Eugen Auerbach were among those who set Kraus texts to music, and not infrequently the printed programs bore the notation "Musik nach Angabe des Vortragenden" ("Music According to the Specifications of the Reciter").

II *Nestroy, Shakespeare, Offenbach*

Karl Kraus must be credited with the modern revival of interest in the Austrian playwright-actor Johann Nestroy, the philosopher-clown and satiric genius of nineteenth-century Vienna. As early as December, 1901, he defended Nestroy in a *Fackel* essay against derogatory remarks made about him by Theodor Herzl. *Nestroy und die Nachwelt (Nestroy and Posterity),* the address which Kraus gave in the Grosser Musikvereinssaal on the fiftieth anniversary of Nestroy's death in 1912, was printed in the *Fackel* in May of that year and appeared as a pamphlet a month later.[13] In it Kraus called his contemporaries "denizens of an age which has lost the ability to be a posterity"[14] and eulogized "a spirit that has been dead for fifty years and still is not alive. . . . In the fifty years since his death, Nestroy's spirit has experienced things which encourage it to go on living. It is wedged in among the paunches of all professions, gives monologues, and laughs metaphysically."[15] It is obvious that Kraus saw a kindred spirit in the dramatist, the first German-language satirist to employ the diversity and the ambiguities of language as a springboard for his satirical sallies. "Nestroy is the first German satirist in whose works language reflects on things," Kraus wrote. "He releases language from paralysis, and for every phrase it yields him a thought. . . . In Nestroy there is so much literature that the theater balks and he has to take the actor's place. He can do so, for this is written dramatic art."[16] Kraus's conviction that Nestroy's use of the Viennese dialect, contrasted with sections in High German, was an artistic device rather than a crutch later led to a basic disagreement with, and even estrangement from, his biographer Leopold Liegler, who proposed to tamper with Nestroy's texts by transcribing them into a stylized Viennese dialect.

With his essays, adaptations, and recitations Kraus initiated a veritable Nestroy renaissance. In January, 1923, he began his first Nestroy cycle with readings of nine plays in his adaptation; later three others were added. On almost one hundred evenings devoted to Nestroy, Kraus presented not only masterpieces like *Der Talisman, Der Zerrissene, Der böse Geist Lumpazivagabundus,* and *Die schlimmen Buben in der Schule,* but also the lesser known works *Eisenbahnheiraten oder Wien, Neustadt, Brünn; Das Notwendige und das Überflüssige* (printed in 1920); *Der konfuse Zauberer* (printed in 1925); *Eine Wohnung ist zu vermieten . . . ; Weder Lorbeerbaum noch Bettelstab; Judith und Holofernes; Tritschtratsch;* and *Liebesgeschichten und Heiratssachen.* Even though these plays constitute only about one-seventh of Nestroy's total output, Kraus succeeded in presenting the playwright in his full stature as a brilliant social satirist and linguistic genius.

Shakespeare was a living force throughout Kraus's life, and references to, and quotations from, the Bard abound in his work. Between

1916 (when he first presented *Die lustigen Weiber von Windsor*) and 1936 Kraus recited his adaptations of thirteen Shakespeare dramas. He planned to issue a four-volume collection of these, but was able to publish only two volumes of *Shakespeare's Dramen. Für Hörer und Leser bearbeitet, teilweise sprachlich erneuert (Shakespeare's Dramas. Arranged for Readers and Listeners, Linguistically Renewed in Part).* The first volume, containing his versions of *King Lear, The Taming of the Shrew* and *The Winter's Tale,* appeared in 1934; a second volume, with *Macbeth, The Merry Wives of Windsor,* and *Troilus and Cressida,* was published the following year. The remaining volumes were to have contained *Love's Labour's Lost, Measure for Measure, Coriolanus, Anthony and Cleopatra, Hamlet,* and *Timon of Athens.* The last-named play was issued separately in 1930, and in 1933 Kraus had published his version of Shakespeare's *Sonnets.*[17]

By including the Bard in his "Theater der Dichtung," Kraus wished to perform an act of linguistic and dramatic restoration and restitution. Once again he was in opposition to those who presented Shakespeare on the stage, including the eminent Vienna Burgtheater, and he felt that he could capture Shakespeare's spirit more fully than other translators. Kraus's versions of Shakespeare are *Nachdichtungen* rather than *Übersetzungen,* free re-creations in the spirit of the original rather than translations. Kraus, who knew little or no English (or any foreign language, for that matter), used existing translations of Shakespeare— the so-called Schlegel-Tieck translation (largely the work of Dorothea Tieck and her husband, Wolf Graf Baudissin) as well as the renderings of Bürger, Schiller, Bodenstedt, Mommsen, Gundolf, and others;[18] for the rest, he was guided by his superior poetic sense and his unerring linguistic instinct. His versions of the *Sonnets,* intended to add Shakespeare to the body of German poetry, were made in programmatic opposition to the *Nachdichtungen* of the German poet Stefan George who, Kraus felt, had done violence to two languages.[19]

Kraus would undoubtedly have appreciated and subscribed to Walter Benjamin's conception of the task of the translator: "A translation, instead of resembling the meaning of the original, must lovingly and in detail incorporate the original's mode of signification. . . . It is the task of the translator to release in his own language that pure language which is under the spell of another, to liberate the language imprisoned in a work in his re-creation of that work."[20] Since his unfamiliarity with the original prevented him from achieving literalness, Kraus must have felt that fidelity was owed to the spirit rather than the letter or the idea of the original work.

One man who disagreed was Richard Flatter, a Viennese attorney who had achieved prominence as a translator of Shakespeare. In a pamphlet issued in 1934, Flatter took issue with Kraus for saying that no non-poet could translate Shakespeare, while a poet need know neither the original nor its language to make a *Dichtung,* a work of literature, out of a mere translation. Flatter states that with his new versions of the first two witches' scenes from *Macbeth,* printed in the *Fackel* of April, 1926,[21] Kraus had unwittingly inspired him to become a Shakespeare translator. Flatter calls the man who thinks he can be more Shakespearean than Shakespeare a "presumptuous dilettante."[22] In reviewing the Shakespeare adaptations, Kraus's American translator Albert Bloch—who had enjoyed Kraus's presentation of *Measure for Measure* in Vienna—points out that they are abridged and sometimes rearranged acting versions and remarks on the "astonishing fitness of the plays as he now issues them for practicable stage-presentation." "With this edition . . . as a guide," writes Bloch, "a conscientious dramaturge, working with loving care, could well take hold of the English originals and, following Karl Kraus scene by scene and line by line, resuscitate them for our stage."[23]

Commenting on Kraus's edition of the *Sonnets,* Bloch feels that if Kraus had known English, his versions would not have been so beautiful. "Perhaps the result is not always immediately identifiable as Shakespeare," the reviewer admits; "certainly it is always undeniably Karl Kraus. . . . Stimulated by the very hopelessness of George's bungling preciosity on the one hand and his equally bungling but obvious efforts, on the other, to follow the original as nearly as possible with literal exactness, Kraus laid hold on this botchwork version and, with the occasional aid of a few of the other existing translations . . . he took the Sonnets . . . and simply rebuilt them, restored them . . . to a figure, firm and final, worthy at last to appear under the name of Shakespeare."[24]

Kraus's special relationship to Offenbach dates back to his boyhood when he attended performances of his operettas at a provincial theater in Baden. "I can imagine," he wrote in *Sprüche und Widersprüche,* "that a young man receives more decisive impressions from the works of Offenbach which he gets to hear in a summer theater than from those classics which he is made to encounter without comprehension in school. His imagination may be stimulated to undertake the outside task of deriving from *La Belle Hélène* the vision of those heroes which the *Iliad* still denies him. It could be that the caricature of the gods will open the true Mount Olympus to him . . ."[25] Elsewhere Kraus called

Offenbach "the greatest musical dramatist of all times," a "genius of gaiety," and "the greatest satirical creator of all ages and cultures." [26]

Kraus preferred operettas to operas. In *Sprüche und Widersprüche,* he called opera nonsense, for it posits the real world and peoples it with men and women who sing when they are jealous, have a headache, or declare war, and even in their dying moments cannot do without coloratura. In an operetta, however, there is a bedrock of absurdity, and singing is accredited as a means of communication; causality is suspended and no rationality expected. In an opera the musical and the theatrical elements conflict, and this juxtaposition is bound to result in a parody, making a mockery of the Wagnerian concept of the *Gesamtkunstwerk* or synthesis of the arts. Only in operetta can action and singing blend to produce such a synthesis, because the operetta has "folly as its premise," [27] with music transfiguring this folly. Operetta nonsense is sheer romanticism based upon intoxication.

In these unromantic times, Kraus points out, operetta has begun to appeal to reason; it has become "psychologized," and there is no more inspired nonsense. "Only now that the genre has adopted reason and put on formal dress will it deserve the contempt which esthetics has always shown it." [28] Kraus was referring to the works of Franz Lehar, Emmerich Kalman, and other contemporaries which he regarded as journalistically false, inane, and harmful. By contrast, Offenbach's operettas not only provide a fine persiflage of grand opera but telling social satire as well. They offer wholesome relaxation for the intellect, dissolve the injustices, perils, and horrors of the modern world into a foolish fairy tale, and turn the dissonance of reality into a sort of gay euphony.

Offenbach assumed ever greater importance in the "Theater of Poetry," and in Kraus's troubled last years he appeared there with his fairy-tale operettas *(Die Reise nach dem Mond, Die Insel Tulipatan, Die Prinzessin von Trapezunt, Fortunios Lied)* rather than his topical satires. With the approval and collaboration of Jacques Brindejont-Offenbach and other members of the composer's family, Kraus presented fourteen operettas. Three of these were performed in new translations by Kraus and appeared in print *(Madame L'Archiduc,* 1927; *Perichole,* 1931; and *Vert-Vert,* 1932).[29] The others *(Die Kreolin, Die Schwätzerin von Saragossa, Die Grossherzogin von Gerolstein, Blaubart, Pariser Leben, Die Seufzerbrücke, Die Briganten,* and those named above) were revisions of existing German versions. Striking omissions are Offenbach's most popular operettas, *The Beautiful Helena* and *Orpheus in the Underworld.*

Kraus put musicologists and cultural historians in his debt by doing pioneer scholarly work in establishing the original or most reliable versions, locating contemporary critiques, and determining the dates of the first performances in Paris and Vienna. In attempting to start an Offenbach renaissance, Kraus not only had to establish Offenbach's greatness and undiminished relevance, but also to contend with incompetent or malevolent *literati,* unscrupulous theater men, and misguided publishers. Among Kraus's greatest satisfactions in his later years was the broadcast, on the Berlin *Funkstunde,* of most of his Offenbach and Shakespeare adaptations. Kraus directed an Offenbach radio cycle between 1930 and 1932, taking charge of the *Wortregie* (verbal direction). His version of *La Perichole* was even performed at the Berlin State Opera in 1931.

One hundred and twenty-three of Kraus's seven hundred recitals were entirely devoted to Offenbach; a number of other evenings included excerpts from Offenbach's works. The printed programs usually carried the following notation: "The presentation of Offenbach's intellectual world of necessity and by choice leaves unfulfilled any claim to a musical interpretation in a strictly technical sense. The music is reproduced without any knowledge of musical notation." Kraus's inability to read music was not compensated for by any great vocal resources. His singing voice was really *Sprechgesang* in the manner of Schönberg or Berg, but it was considerably enhanced by his great intuition and empathy, his rhythmic acuteness, his talent as an imitator, and his pervasive moral fanaticism. In an address before the first performance of *Vert-Vert* in Vienna, Kraus contrasted himself, his accompanist (from 1930 on, Franz Mittler was the regular pianist for the Offenbach evenings), and one janitor with a staff of 972 employed for Reinhardt's Berlin production of the *Tales of Hoffmann.* For these complete operettas Kraus had no rehearsals other than a careful comparison of the text with the music. Paul Rilla commented in 1930 that "the non-musician Kraus makes music not with his throat but with his mind which, if anywhere, is the only appropriate instrument for Offenbach."[30] While musicologists like Paul Amadeus Pisk and writer-scholars like Max Brod were critical of Kraus's musical interpretations, the consensus of musicians was probably expressed by the composer Ernst Křenek:

One listens intently for three and one-half hours and at the end is sorry that it is over. . . . This is due not only to the dialogue, which has been enriched or brought up to date organically, with every sentence hitting home satirically, or to the brilliant additions to the *couplets,* but primarily to the fact that the presentation makes the entire work come to life dramatically. An uncommon stage sense is at work here, and the creative scenic imagination of the reciter produces, as if by magic, a fully alive theatrical picture only by means of a voice and a few gestures. Musicians owe Kraus a particular debt of gratitude for leaving the musical text inviolate." [31]

Křenek's reference is to the *Zusatzstrophen,* the additional stanzas which Kraus interpolated in the *couplets* and songs of numerous Offenbach and Nestroy works. These appeared in book form in 1931 under the title *Zeitstrophen (Topical Stanzas).* This book is a veritable "Krausiad" in that it presents an unabashedly Kraus-centered waxworks of contemporary figures in politics and the arts, lampooning personalities and conditions in the Austrian republic. The first section is devoted to Nestroy and contains ingenious additions to eleven works in the dramatist's style and spirit. Here the topical stanzas are inserted between the original ones, while in other cases they continue a *couplet.* There are references to Békessy and Schober, the press and psychoanalysis, Křenek's then controversial jazz opera *Jonny spielt auf,* the nude dances of Josephine Baker ("In Vienna we don't like foreigners who have already lost their shirts"),[32] the banking crisis, tourism, politics, and musical intrigues. The Offenbach section also contains new material for eleven works. "Whores have been barred from the Ringstrasse," says Kraus in *Die Seufzerbrücke,* "but an older whore is unaffected by the prohibition, plying her trade on Fichtegasse" [33] (the location of the building of the *Neue Freie Presse,* off the Ringstrasse). In a *Zeitstrophe* for *Pariser Leben,* Kraus intimates that he is thinking of leaving Vienna: "The denoument which will presumably please all: I go, Schober stays, Békessy returns." [34] Perhaps Kraus will be offered better things if he returns as a stranger some day. Since Social Democratic leaders in charge of culture have claimed that Offenbach was outdated, Kraus triumphantly sings: "There resounds what has faded, what's passé now holds sway." [35]

III   *The Dream Plays*

"I open for you the magic realm of Offenbach's dream music," wrote Kraus in *Zeitstrophen.*[36] His view of Offenbach's greatness may have been shaped by his conception of dreams. For Kraus the dream was a most valuable possession of a man and artist, and the answer of the dreamer, the whole man, to the questions which a waking, fragmentary man is unable to solve. The dream is a basic, ever recurrent motif in Kraus's works (the witty prose sketch "Der Traum ein Wiener Leben,"[37] a nightmare about Vienna's public conveyances, is a case in point); in a number of his poems Kraus depicted the relationship between waking and dreaming.[38] In Kraus's dreams, friends occasionally become foes, but he may also see his foes in a light which makes them too worthy to be enemies.

Traumstück (Dream Play), a one-act verse drama written during Christmas of 1922 and published the following year, appeared on a number of Kraus's recitals. In this surrealistic dramatic fantasy, lyrical and grotesque elements intermingle. Kraus himself described it as "a series of visions of dozing and dreaming, born of the experiences of the war, the horrors of the postwar period, bad life and bad knowledge, newspapers, psychoanalysis, love, language, and dreams themselves."[39] The play opens with a pessimistic monologue of the poet sitting in his writing chair. His vigor and passion have availed him nothing, and his vital questions have elicited only a sterile echo; force overpowers nature, matter smothers the spirit, and the world is indifferent. The somnolent poet, at once the driver and the driven, has visions: a dead soldier, "the model of this bloody age";[40] a general, a technician, and a journalist, "the bloody henchmen of baseness";[41] a tubercular child whose parents and siblings were killed or hurt in the war; Valuta (Foreign Exchange) and Zinsfuss (Interest Rate) dancing a foxtrot.

The poet hopes for clarity, strength, and fresh impulses from the dream world. As the landscape dissolves, "Die Psychoanalen" (the Psychoanals) appear. In a long chorus they identify themselves as killers of dreams, blackeners of beauty, creators of symbols, interpreters of sneezes, thrivers on the subconscious, compilers of complexes, exhibitors of inhibitions, purveyors of neuroses, maskers of their own deficiencies, people to whom even Goethe's poems are nothing but bad repressions: "There remains our *codex;* the moon is a *podex;* the comet, a member."[42] After the "psychoanals" have disintegrated, a picture leaves its frame in the poet's room and briefly appears as Imago; the speech of this character indicates that Kraus has once more erected a memorial to Annie Kalmar. A newspaper appears and The Dream speaks to the poet about it: It is all right for you to wake up; here is your reality, your inspiration, here are your victories; this is the material you can master and overcome; the same linguistic power that turns gnats into elephants will reduce elephants to gnats; it is given to you to live in the Word, and thus you will outlive life itself. The Poet is awakened by rug-beating outside; this sound, so familiar to inhabitants of Viennese apartment houses, is the signal for a rebellion of those without rights. In his closing soliloquy, the poet states that the dream has brightened his cloudy day and clarified his mission for him.

The legacy of Annie Kalmar also shaped the little one-act play *Traumtheater (Dream Theater),* which is dedicated to her memory and appeared in 1924. In it Kraus has the beloved actress "play love" for him so that his love might be purged of jealousy. This improvisatory philosophical-dramatic vignette consists of very brief scenes in both prose and verse. Manfred Georg has described it as "a tender symphony of the recognition of the nature of theater." [43] At the beginning, the Director and the Poet converse in the latter's room. "My works bloom in her mouth," says the Poet. "One cannot overestimate a woman enough." [44] To the Director's doubts that an actress can have enough left to be a woman, the Poet replies that he once knew a female in whom the actress and the woman were one: "Only a step from child to queen—and in between, prostitute and lady in every shape." [45] The Director admits that he could enjoy this phenomenon if there were not a "cook in the witches' kitchen"; [46] but the brain of an actress is like blotting paper that absorbs any writing.

When the Director leaves, the Poet falls asleep. The scene shifts to a dressing room in which the Actress and the Poet converse. She: "How strange that we can work magic as soon as we step onto the boards. All it takes is some greasepaint." [47] Poet: "I nourish you as the most beautiful of the flames which have emanated from my thoughts. . . . You have played Titania, queen of the elves, and tomorrow you will caress an ass." [48] In her boudoir, the Actress receives the visit of the Old Ass who always sits in the first row and would not mind having an affair, provided his wife does not get wind of it. The Actress is attracted to him as a tender father symbol and an experienced man. Back in the dressing room, the Poet accuses her of wanting new things. Once she is through with the old ass, she will have young men from the standing-room section. Actress: "Only you have me. . . . The world is down below, ours is the stage!" [49] Poet: "Oh, if only all those who kiss you knew that it was not really You!" [50]

In the next scene, Walter, a high school student, comes in search of an autograph and gets her love. Following his monologue on the set, just before the actress' cue, the Poet awakens. In the final scene, the Director and the Poet converse again. The Poet reveals that he dreamt she played a stellar part and he a minor role. "We were both lost—she in the world, and I in thought." [51] "That theater and dreams are related," says the Director, "is certainly not proved by the fact that you brought the theater into your dream, but it might be proved by your taking the dream into the theater." [52]

IV Cloudcuckooland

Kraus regarded his reading of *Wolkenkuckucksheim (Cloudcuckooland)*, a "Phantastic Verse Play in Three Acts," before an audience of workers as a most beautiful and most fitting celebration of the Austrian Republic. Based on Aristophanes' *Ornithes (The Birds)*, in particular on Schinck's translation into German, the play was written unusually quickly—from the end of June to the middle of July, 1923—and dedicated to Berthold Viertel. The first reading of the play, an "apotheosis of the republican idea" [53], took place in Vienna on November 1, 1923; it has never been performed on the stage. Basing himself on an old tradition in the Viennese folk theater, the travesty of classical motifs, Kraus retained some of Aristophanes' characters and, in the earlier part, his plot outline as well.

Pisthetairos (Pisthetaerus) and Euelpides, two Athenians who decide to emigrate because they find conditions in their native city unbearable, appear in Kraus's play as Ratefreund and Hoffegut. Epops, the hoopoe that once was a human, appears as Wiedehopf, the ruler of the birds' domain, and his doorkeeper Troglodytes is Zaunschlüpfer, the wren. Prokne (Procné), the nightingale mate of Epops, is another character retained by Kraus. When the hoopoe says of the Athens which his visitors are complaining about "Selbst Trübsal blasen sie dort fesch und munter/und der Athener, sagt man, geht nicht unter" [54] ("There they beat even the doldrums snappily and merrily,/ and they say that an Athenian never goes to ruin"), this adaptation of a popular Viennese ditty makes it plain that the city satirized is Vienna.

Upon the appearance of the birds, Hoffegut thinks that the Eisvogel (kingfisher) is directly from the Prater (Eisvogel being the name of a restaurant there). The visitors suggest the formation of a preeminent bird-state called Cloudcuckooland (in Aristophanes this is Nephelococcygia) between the earth and the abode of the gods, where the sacrificial vapors intended for the gods can be intercepted. The Athenians defend themselves against the pecking birds with cooking utensils. The visitors from Athens tell the birds how ancient and important they are: they were the lords of the universe long before the

Olympians and now have a chance to re-establish their supremacy. Idioms in which bird images or metaphors figure prominently are cited: a chicken to pluck, ostrich policy, swan song, proud as a peacock. The birds can take the place of the gods, but they will have to stop eating the seeds and act as their own scarecrows. In Aristophanes, the birds' chorus gives reasons why men should worship the birds as gods; in Kraus, the Athenians do so.

In Act Two the Athenians have become birds in the bird city and make fun of each other's strange appearance. The Dompfaff (bullfinch) appears as a priest and prays to the olympian birds; the birds, it turns out, have eaten up all the offerings. A journalist appears, bent upon interviewing even before the official inauguration, and offers to assist with a new paper, *Der freie Vogel (The Free Bird)*. In Aristophanes, typical Athenian pests appear at this point, eager to offer their services and ply their trades; Kraus substitutes the coffeehouse culture of Austria. Neutöner (an avant-garde poet, that is, an Expressionist) appears: surely the birds need a new *Weltanschauung* to go with their new city, as well as someone to speak the prologue at the inauguration. (He has emigrated because the waiter in the Café Central refused to extend him any more credit.)

Subsequently, Weltfreund arrives and delivers a parody of Werfel's poetic sentiments.[55] He wishes to explore the ethereal world of the birds and add it to his cosmic visions. Bursting with universal love, he wants Ratefreund to take him under his wing. A *Hellseher* (Clairvoyant) enters and warns that the bird city will be built on air. The Falcon has espied two architects debating whether duckbills ought to be decorated, the peacock needs new wallpaper patterns, and nests should be black and white boxes; doesn't a cultured bird need ornaments? An Ornithosophist argues that theosophy and anthroposophy are passé and the time has come for *Ornithosophie,* the third Sophie.

A Psychoanalyst is advised by Ratefreund: "You're at the wrong address. Someone should take him to Sophocles."[56] The analyst has an *Ungeratener Sohn* in tow, a would-be parricide who wants to get rid of his father in the manner of birds—"a typical case of bird neurosis!"[57] A Commissar of the League of Nations appears to bid the new state be thrifty, saying that the building of a wall was wasteful. The Dove returns and reports on the conditions prevailing on earth: people there are busy acting like birds; they live in a world of *Blätter* (leaves/newspapers), millions of *Federn* (feathers/pens) are in use. Blood and money are the people's main interests, and they have no use for the dove of peace. They dance on all graves and volcanoes, parrot what they read in the papers, and behave like parasites. Their bird mentality is expressed in names like Adler (Eagle), Hahn (Rooster), Rab (Raven), Falk (Falcon), Specht (Woodpecker), Storch (Stork), Strauss (Ostrich), Fink (Finch), Wachtel (Quail), and Sperber (Sparrow-Hawk).

Inspired by this intelligence, Ratefreund is ready to declare a *Verteidigungskrieg,* a defensive war. Iris, the messenger of the gods, appears; she has gone astray in her flight from Zeus to the human race in an effort to persuade them to sacrifice to the gods again. When Ratefreund says that "all birds will be mobilized [*einrückend gemacht*] to fight in the battle of the gods. . . . Up and at 'em! . . . The crown is mine . . . by the grace of God," [58] it is clear that the stage is set for the Last Days of Birdkind.

In Act Three Kraus parts company with Aristophanes. In wartime the Turkey chides the Sparrow for his antiwar sentiments: "You traitor, keep silent *in dieser grossen Zeit*!" [59] He calls him a *Nörgler,* a pacifist and defeatist, tells him that war is a "steel bath," and mouths martial slogans and patriotic clichés like *durchhalten* [60] (see it through). Human mores have really affected the birds. Four cocks make like the jaded playboy officers at the Sirk-Ecke; the Capercailzie and the Guineafowl flirt like members of high society; there are special editions of *Der freie Vogel;* the Subscriber and the Patriot converse, and Flamingo von Fahnenfeld, the military leader, appears and speaks of stabs in the back, strategic withdrawals, and such. Ratefreund tells the birds that they deserve "a place in the sun" and delivers himself of such Francisco-Josephinian sentiments as "Es was sehr schön, es hat mich sehr gefreut" and "Ich habe alles reiflich erwogen" as well as Wilhelmian gems like "Ich hab es nicht gewollt." [61]

The Falcon having brought bad tidings, two helpers arrive from earth, identify themselves as *Legitimisten,* and offer to reform the monarchy and thus save it from downfall. They discuss the loyalty of various birds, for example, the imperial eagle. Repainting birds with different colors might do it in some cases. One of the helpers suggests that nationalism and racism be introduced and all nonindigenous elements be driven out; the hooked cross could serve as a symbol and poison gas might be used. Ratefreund agrees that a combination of chemistry and romanticism will do the trick—and for the rest, Wotan will easily handle Zeus. At that point, Wiedehopf receives a telegram from the Foreign Office in Athens, signed by Pericles, who requests the extradition of Ratefreund and Hoffegut—those notorious confidence men who are wanted for tax delinquency and on suspicion of monarchistic agitation—as well as the unimpeded passage of the sacrificial vapors. Wiedehopf removes the crown from Rategut's head: "You are human. For you taught us to hate." [62] Ratefreund's response is "Mir bleibt doch nichts erspart" [63] ("I am spared nothing"). After a brief rejoicing statement by the Chorus, the Lark ends the play with a Shakespearean solo. All have been dreaming; the confusion of purpose and function is now ended; the birds do not want to be worshiped by men as gods; no more violence or wars; "we dreamt of power, we live as republicans . . . *Nie wieder Krieg*!" [64]

CHAPTER 8

"The Word Passed Away . . ."

I Revolutionary and Reactionary

KRAUS'S SATIRE is basically oriented toward culture and not toward politics in any specific and narrow sense. He was not a *homo politicus*, but it would not be entirely accurate to call him apolitical. On the very first page of the first issue of the *Fackel*, Kraus declared that he was not a *"parteimässig Verschnittener"*—a man castrated along party lines. Too exclusive to be a joiner ("According to the census, Vienna has 2,030,834 inhabitants. That is, 2,030,833 souls and myself"),[1] too dynamic to make any lasting political commitment or alignment, Kraus can best be described as a relatively apolitical man with an *ad hoc* attitude toward politics based on personalities rather than parties.

The Socialist sympathies of the young Kraus are expressed in *A Crown for Zion* and other writings of the turn of the century, but later Kraus became increasingly disillusioned with the world of politics. In 1906 Robert Scheu addressed an open letter to Kraus in which he questioned the latter's rejection of the *Wahlreform*, the Social Democrats' campaign to secure universal suffrage (which came to fruition the following year). Instead of practicing what he had apparently preached, Kraus seemed to have retreated into an ivory tower of estheticism. In his reply, Kraus said that his apolitical orientation was based on the recognition that the moving forces of his time were not to be found in parliaments but in newspaper offices; his studied ignorance as a nonpolitical man bade him be silent. Teaching workers to appreciate the arts would only serve to perpetuate bourgeois ideals. To Scheu's statement that Kraus dreamt of an aristocratic leadership which no longer existed, Kraus replied that he had as much of a right to be utopian as anyone else, and, for the rest, "If I am supposed to choose the lesser of two evils, I shall choose neither."[2]

After the world war, Kraus's interest in politics was revived. He supported the republican revolution, and his short-lived hope that the dawn of a great democratic era was at hand led him, in February, 1919, to appeal "an Alle, die die Wahl haben" ("to all who have a choice *or* have the vote") to vote for the Social Democrats; his appeal was renewed the following year. Kraus also modified his earlier stand by giving readings to large groups of workers under the auspices of the Social Democrats' cultural department, which was headed by David Bach; yet the powers that be soon felt that his material was too complex or otherwise unsuitable for his proletarian audiences.

Following his spectacular departure from the Catholic Church in 1922–23, the majority party increasingly looked upon Kraus as an *enfant terrible.* What was regarded as his carping criticism of Social Democratic causes and conditions—a criticism prompted by the impatience of an idealist—led to counterpolemics by younger politicians like Oskar Pollak, the future editor-in-chief of the *Arbeiterzeitung,* notably in the pages of the monthly *Der Kampf;* and eventually the *Arbeiterzeitung* joined the cabal of silence about Kraus. It was felt that Kraus had no understanding of modern economics and science, that he disregarded the achievements and promises of technology.[3] Kraus, for his part, felt that the Social Democrats were neglecting spiritual-moral values while fighting for material betterment. After Friedrich Austerlitz' death in 1931, Kraus's enemies in the ranks of the party gained the upper hand. The Social Democrats' failure to join the fight against Békessy until it was almost won,[4] as well as their fawning obeisance to Schober on the third anniversary of the July events, contributed to Kraus's isolation and set the stage for the dilemma of his last years. "I am a member of no party, but view them all with equal disdain," he wrote in 1931. "Without looking to the left or to the right, my politics are revolutionary and reactionary at the same time—in short, I am what the idiots of all parties call an *Eigenbrötler* [a loner]."[5]

Writing in 1931, the Marxist critic Walter Benjamin pointed out that originally Kraus's resources were bourgeois virtues; only in the scuffle did they acquire their combative appearance. "This great bourgeois character turned comedian, this preserver of the Goethean linguistic heritage who had become a polemicist, this blameless man of honor went berserk. This had to happen, because he planned to start changing the world with his class, in his hometown Vienna."[6] Kraus's seemingly strange alternation between reactionary theory and revolutionary practice, his feeling that the contradiction in his attitude—from Dreyfus to Dollfuss—was simply the contradiction inherent in the world is succinctly expressed in his epigrammatic poem

My Inconsistency

Where life to their lie was subjugated
I was a revolutionary.
Where nature in favor of norms was berated
I was a revolutionary.
My bond with man's suffering I have confessed.

Where freedom to hollow phrases was suited
I was a reactionary.
Where art with their artifice was polluted
I was a reactionary.
And back to the source I have retrogressed.[7]

II   The Third Walpurgis Night

"Mir fällt zu Hitler nichts ein"[8] ("I cannot think of anything to say about Hitler"). This is the striking first sentence of *Die Dritte Walpurgisnacht,* a book which did not appear in Kraus's lifetime. As it turned out, the apocalyptic visionary did have a great deal to say about Hitler and Hitlerism. That sentence, the germ cell of the misunderstandings and conflicts which marked and marred Kraus's last years, may indeed be indicative of resignation, but it is even more a hyperbolic, heuristic device for depicting the witches' sabbath of the time. A convincing interpretation has been suggested by Kurt Wolff: "In hell one does not speak of the devil."[9] *Die Dritte Walpurgisnacht*—the title refers to both parts of *Faust* as well as to the Third Reich—was written in the late spring and summer of 1933; it had been set in type and corrected to appear as Nos. 888—907 of *Die Fackel* when Kraus decided not to publish it—for fear that hell might retaliate by unleashing its furies on innocent people. There had been no *Fackel* for ten months when No. 888 appeared in October, 1933; its four pages contained a funeral oration on Adolf Loos and Kraus's last poem:

Man frage nicht, was all die Zeit ich machte.
Ich bleibe stumm;
und sage nicht, warum.
Und Stille gibt es, da die Erde krachte.
Kein Wort, das traf;
Man spricht nur aus dem Schlaf.
Und träumt von einer Sonne, welche lachte.
Es geht vorbei;
nachher war's einerlei.
Das Wort entschlief, als jene Welt erwachte.[10]

(Do not ask what I have been doing all this time. I remain silent and do not say why. And it is still since the earth cracked. No word hit home; one speaks only in one's sleep and dreams of a sun which used to laugh. It will pass; afterwards it was all the same. The word passed away when that world awoke.)

Bert Brecht was among the few who understood. In a poem entitled "On the Significance of the Ten-Line Poem in No. 888 of the *Fackel*," he wrote:

> When the Third Reich had been founded
> Only a short message came from the eloquent one.
> In a ten-line poem
> He raised his voice to complain
> That it was not adequate.
>
> When the eloquent one excused himself
> That his voice had failed him,
> Silence stepped forward to the judgment seat,
> Removed her veil
> And revealed herself as a witness.[11]

Yet by the time this poem appeared in the *Festschrift* for Kraus's sixtieth birthday, Brecht had responded to Kraus's support of the Austrian government's repressive measures during the riots of February, 1934, and its proscription of the Social Democratic party by writing a supplementary poem entitled "About the Quick Fall of the Good Innocent":

> He testified against those whose lips had been sealed
> And broke his staff over those who had been killed.
> He praised the murderers. He accused the murdered . . .
>
> What an age, we said, shuddering,
> When the man of good will but no understanding
> Cannot even wait to perform his misdeed
> Until praise for his good deed has reached him! . . .[12]

Issue No. 889 of the *Fackel* appeared in July, 1934, containing "Nachrufe auf Karl Kraus" ("Obituaries on Karl Kraus")—often rancorous critical statements from the emigrant press that accused Kraus of political complicity with the forces of reaction and berated him for lack of solidarity with anti-Nazi writers. Major portions of *Die Dritte Walpurgisnacht*—those pertaining to the situation in Austria specifically—are contained in the 315-page *Fackel* Nos. 890–905; it appeared a few days before the assassination of Chancellor Engelbert

Dollfuss on July 25, 1934. (On a poster announcing that issue's title, "Warum *Die Fackel* nicht erscheint" ["Why the *Fackel* Does Not Appear"], an "understanding troglodyte" scribbled the words "Because he values his life.") This *Fackel* is in three parts: a letter from the publishers to an imaginary correspondent explaining Kraus's refusal to polemicize against Hitler; a letter by Kraus to his publisher; and a poem, "Ad Spectatores," written after the murder of the storm troopers' leader Ernst Röhm and expressing the hope that the monsters would kill one another off.

"One ought to read this book as a document of the year 1933, not as a work of literature" [13], writes Wilhelm Alff in a historical essay included in a recent special edition of *Die Dritte Walpurgisnacht.* Representing Kraus's viewpoint, Heinrich Fischer disagrees as a matter of principle,[14] because annotating Kraus's work and placing it in the context of his time (something that Frank Field has done for all of Kraus's work) reduces the satirist's apocalyptic vision to the material plane and takes it back to that topicality based on concrete subject matter which Kraus always strove to escape. Kraus felt that his work would increase in clarity and significance as the specific occasion, as the political, historical, literary, personal details receded into the background; only then could the symbolic, timeless, paradigmatic quality of his work come to the fore. Never interested in merely providing "information," he felt that language would overcome the obstacle of a reader's unfamiliarity with circumstances and details.

In September, 1933, a reader of the *Fackel* sent Kraus a copy of the Lessing parable "The Shepherd and the Nightingale": " 'Do sing, dear nightingale!' said a shepherd to the silent singer one lovely spring evening. 'Alas,' replied the nightingale, 'the frogs are so loud that I have lost all desire to sing. Don't you hear them?' 'Of course I hear them,' said the shepherd, 'but only because you are silent.' " Kraus replied that this parable did not apply to the *Fackel.* The nightingale's song would have had to include the croaking of the frogs, and among the shepherds there were many who liked that noise and thought that singing and croaking could be combined. Also, the noise of the frogs was something natural, whereas the doings of the Austrian Social Democrats were the most unnatural thing imaginable. A nightingale's song could not possibly drown out this cacophony.[15]

It is against this background that Kraus's work in his last years must be viewed. Is linguistic or literary art still possible when a brutal power structure—one that is inimical to the spirit—has assumed absolute control? That is the anguished question which Kraus had to ask himself in the early and middle 1930s. "Is that which has been done to the spirit still a concern of the spirit?" [16] he wondered in *Die Dritte Walpurgisnacht*. Like modern Germany's greatest satirist, the Berlin-born Kurt Tucholsky, who also fell silent in 1933,[17] Kraus believed that "force is no object of polemics, madness no object of satire." [18] Kraus realized that he had committed himself with his vision of the last days of mankind. Since he continued to be more receptive than productive, he was subject to astonishment at the return of the monstrous in ever heightened forms, for the perpetrators of the new horrors obviously were not characters from an operetta. He based himself in vain on the Shakespearean formula which combines pain and solace:

> O gods! Who is't can say: "I am at the worst"?
> I am worse than e'er I was.
> And worse I may be yet: the worst is not
> So long as we can say "This is the worst."

—King Lear, IV, 1

The entire *Walpurgisnacht* seems like a desperate rear-guard action; it is the rambling monologue of a worried man who talks incessantly in an effort to keep the demons at bay, the thrashing about of a man desperately trying to keep afloat in the rampaging waters of a polluted river.[19] Attempting to plumb the demonic depths of the Third Reich through language, to write about "a dictatorship which today is in command of everything but language" [20], Kraus comments on the early boycotts, excesses, and sadistic practices of the Nazi regime and minutely analyzes its slogans and poems. Surely no one but Kraus would have noticed—or commented upon—that "Deutschland erwache" ("Germany Awake") and "Juda verrecke" [21] ("Perish Juda") lacked commas, being commands rather than wishes expressed in the subjunctive. Neologisms or aberrant words like *Willensbildung, Kultureinheit, Einstellung, Auftrieb, Auswertung, Auflockerung* supply stunning evidence of the incommensurability of Kraus's linguistic world with the world across the border. A close look is taken at some of the intellectuals who have committed treason against the spirit by making common cause with Hitlerism within months of its assumption of power: Martin Heidegger, Oswald Spengler, Rudolf Binding, Gottfried Benn, Richard Strauss, and Wilhelm Furtwängler.[22]

While Kraus had not changed his mind about the activities of Jews in journalism, industry, high finance, and public life generally, he was well aware of the dilemma in which the National Socialists found themselves in regard to his person and work. His books had not been included in the big bonfires of May, 1933, and he remembered that Jörg Lanz von Liebenfels ("the man who gave Hitler his ideas," according to a recent study) [23] had twenty years previously hailed Kraus as the savior of the *Ariogermanentum,* the German Aryan spirit. Kraus noted with interest that in the spring of 1933 the *Neue Freie Presse* had assured its readers that no Jew was being harmed in Germany. Kraus himself was keenly alive to the plight of the Jews. "Jewry has, in many cases, surrendered to an intransigent *Deutschtum* [Germanic mentality], with no thanks and little recognition from their taskmasters." [24] Jews did not realize that when submissiveness does no good, one might as well display courage. "National-German Jews" were an abomination, yet such an association had issued a book entitled *The Horror Propaganda Is a Lying Propaganda,* and, according to its chairman, the fact that Jews were being treated very unjustly by their non-Jewish *Volksgenossen* (fellow nationals) must not deflect them from their straight path—the integration into the German body politic and German culture.

Kraus regarded statements that Jews invented the microphone and discovered cathode rays, the gonococcus, and other things as futile and pointless. "Jews with the urge to be *nationaldeutsch*," he wrote, "are a combination of two inferiority complexes that ought to be repressed." [25] About the Nazis' silly search for "Aryan" grandmothers, Kraus said: "An ounce of intelligence might be recognized in the hope that one will discover a Jewish grandmother—a windfall which would leave some hope for this generation." [26] In Oberammergau the traditional Passion Play was to be presented with Christ as a blond, blue-eyed man, with his faithful disciples of Aryan-Germanic appearance, and only Judas as a pronounced Jewish type; perhaps the play would soon be devoted to Hitler, the "Nazirene." [27] Commenting on the canard that Hitler himself had Jewish blood in his veins, Kraus wrote: "It is a bad habit of the Jews to claim everything for themselves and, as the ultimate disparagement, to assert that someone belongs to their community." [28]

In the second part of *Die Dritte Walpurgisnacht,* Kraus discusses Austria with genuine concern about Germany's pressure on, and threat to, what he now unequivocally identifies as *his* country. In an epigram entitled "Anschluss," he had commented on the Social Democrats' earlier quest for a union with Germany: "What would I be doing in Germany? I am not *angeschlossen* [attached] to Austria as yet." [29]

Now, however, he leaves no doubt that he is in Austria's corner. For the first time he finds it possible "to recognize the congruence of individual interests which aim at preserving the possibility to live and work with the will of the state."[30] This state was under the guidance of the Christian Socialist chancellor Dollfuss, and Kraus admitted that he was incapable of any satiric impulse against him. The Social Democrats, on the other hand, have debated and vacillated while the National Socialists have acted. "Since the invention of politics to the detriment of mankind there has not been anything as stupid as the behavior of the Austrian Social Democrats."[31] Heinrich Fischer recalls Kraus telling him in 1933: "As long as there is Hitler, with stand-up coffins, concentration camps, pillories, the murdering of Jews, everything else is unimportant, and all talk about 'clerico-Fascism' only is proof that many of my best adherents have surrendered to the power of newspaper clichés and political slogans. I am being asked to attack Major Fey, a Dollfuss man, because he is a 'bloodhound.' But if a bloodhound is trained to attack Hitler, then even this bloodhound is a friend of mine."[32] As Wilhelm Alff has pointed out, *Die Dritte Walpurgisnacht*—or the *Fackel* which appeared at the end of July, 1934—may be read as "a depiction of what the Dollfuss government was saving Austria from."[33]

III *An Occupant of the "Safe Sentence Structure"*

"Beim Weltuntergang will ich privatisieren"[34] ("When the end of the world comes, I want to live in retirement")—this was Kraus's basic reaction to the spooks of the third Walpurgis Night. The assassination of Dollfuss was a severe blow to him. By that time Kraus had realized that his unintended "activism" had assured him of the kind of topical interest as a purveyor of utilitarian "opinion" which had always been anathema to him. Many of his erstwhile leftist adherents, some of them turned Communist, now rejected him. Of necessity the *Fackel* lost readers and became a losing proposition, while the "Theater of Poetry" lost listeners. But Kraus did not wish to keep a following on the basis of intellectual compromise; in fact, he wanted to reduce the readership of the *Fackel* to those who were interested not only in the problems of the day but in Shakespeare as well: "Was darüber ist, das ist vom Übel"[35] ("Whatsoever is more, cometh of evil"—Matthew 5, 37).

Kraus's epigrammatic "Request to Admirers"—"Nicht Ruhm, nur Ruh . . ."[36] ("Not fame, but quiet")—was particularly relevant now that he was preparing to "live in the safe sentence structure" *(im sicheren Satzbau wohnen).*[37] Following a nineteen-month hiatus, Kraus resumed his public readings in November, 1934, and devoted his *Theater der Dichtung* primarily to Shakespeare, Nestroy, and Offenbach. A book with the title *Die Sprache* had been announced for the spring of 1933, but it did not appear until 1937–posthumously. In essays and glosses on many aspects of language Kraus deals with the "immeasurable and always undeveloped area of *Sprachlehre.*"[38] *Sprachlehre* here denotes more than grammar or stylistics; it must be seen as Kraus's somewhat pathetic and quixotic attempt to pit the power of the word against the power of the sword. Ernst Křenek's reminiscence is pertinent in this connection: "When people were excited about the Japanese bombardment of Shanghai and I found Karl Kraus occupied with one of his famous comma problems, he said something like this: 'I know that all this is senseless when the house is afire. But for as long as it is at all possible, I have to do it, for if the people whose duty it is had seen to it that all commas were in their right places, Shanghai would not be burning.' "[39]

In *Pro domo et mundo* he had written: "Even thirty years after my death I shall care more about a comma being in the right place than about the dissemination of the rest of the text."[40] *Die Sprache,* containing mostly pieces written since 1921, furnishes ample evidence of Kraus's conviction that no amount of attention to syntax, diction, punctuation, and the finest points of linguistic usage—including even misprints—could ever be excessive. Glosses on the differences between *verbieten* and *verbitten, wieso kommt es?* and *wie kommt es?, nur noch* and *nur mehr, als* and *wie, der* and *welcher, zumuten* and *zutrauen* are not mere disquisitions on linguistic usage and differ greatly from what may be found in the German equivalents of Fowler's *Modern English Usage.* These pieces are profound, highly charged, often witty and devastating, with a bedrock of consistent morality clearly in evidence. Yet Kraus realized that "it is quite safe to define style as that which the reader does not understand"[41], that "nothing is harder than to communicate about language with people who speak or even write it"[42], and that he was writing for "a people which will soon no longer have a language to assure the world that it cannot perish."[43] Kraus's advice to his remaining followers was to be courageous and devote themselves to *Sprachlehre.* The formation of language seminars was a favorite idea of his toward the end of his life. "The more barbaric and callous the world around him became," writes J. P. Stern, "the more insistent his tone and his claim that he held the whole world captive in a phrase. And the more insistent his claim, the more desperate his realization that the age was past hope and past praying for, that his immensely subtle and varied vision was lost on it." [44]

Karl Kraus's sixtieth birthday was celebrated with a musical-literary matinee which included the showing of the new film, *Karl Kraus liest aus eigenen Schriften (Karl Kraus Reading from His Works)*, several articles, and–a bit belatedly–the publication of *Stimmen über Karl Kraus zum 60. Geburtstag* with tributes by Knut Hamsun, Henri Barbusse, Karel Čapek, Marcel Ray, Jan Münzer (his French and Czech translators), Alban Berg, Oskar Jellinek (poetic "Thanks of the German Language to Karl Kraus"), and others. Berthold Viertel's elegiac contribution sums up the feelings of those still loyal to Kraus:

Karl Kraus has turned sixty. When we were boys of fourteen . . . we read his *Fackel* while hiding it under our school benches. We never stopped reading it–but now he has stopped writing it. After a lifetime of powerful speech this warner is now silent. For there no longer is anything to warn about. Everything happened the way he knew it beforehand, foresaw and foretold it. All horrors have come to pass–that war and this peace. He has had the harshest fate: to be proved right in such a frightful way. So he finally fell silent, like the prophet Samuel who went up on the mountain and did not look down upon the lost city. The harshest fate, the fate of the prophet who is confirmed by misfortune. They were all writing feuilletons when Karl Kraus started writing his *mene tekel*. Today they continue to write their feuilletons, but Karl Kraus is silent. What?! He has turned sixty? So much the worse for all of us. He has lived to be sixty in vain. What good is it to eulogize him now? The future will eulogize him. Our downfall at least does one thing for him: it accredits his thought and his writing. The future will make use of it. [45]

Kraus's death on June 12, 1936, at the end of a long period of physical and spiritual exhaustion, mercifully saved him from witnessing the Nazi rape of Austria, the desecration of his apartment and of the *Fackel* publishing house, the destruction of his library and the Lanyi collection of Krausiana, the deaths of his friends Richard Lanyi and Philipp Berger in concentration camps, and untold other horrors. The last word on the last page of the last issue of the *Fackel*–one in which Kraus continued to attack the Social Democrats–is "Trottel" (idiot). As J. P. Stern has pointed out, this intimates "most movingly and powerfully . . . the despair at a vision, at once noble and merciless, overthrown by the base reality of an age. No other age could have yielded such a vision, no other age would have destroyed it so cruelly." [46] Kraus saw himself as an end product when he wrote: "The satiric artist is at the end of a development which denies itself to art. He is its product and its hopeless opposite. He organizes the flight of the spirit from mankind. . . . After him the deluge." [47]

"In the twelve years that followed the accession of Hitler to power in Germany," writes Frank Field, "things were to happen that surpassed the most pessimistic insights of the satirist: the building of the concentration camp at Buchenwald around Goethe's beech tree, and the processions that took place into the extermination chambers of Auschwitz while elsewhere in the camp the orchestra played selections from Viennese light music—all this only becomes a little more explicable after reading the work of Kraus." [48] Bert Brecht probably summed up Kraus's significance most succinctly by saying "When the age died by its own hand, he was that hand." [49] In his inability to save his time by turning his fellow men to the sources of spiritual power in their cultural heritage, in his fighting a rear-guard action in behalf of the spirit in a dying age, in his relentless, truculent criticism of so many aspects of human nature, Karl Kraus may have been a failure. But surely he was one of the grandest failures in world literature.

Notes and References

Preface

1. Erich Heller, "Karl Kraus." In *The Disinherited Mind* (New York: Farrar, Straus & Cudahy, 1957), p. 239.

2. Friedell, *A Cultural History of the Modern Age,* (New York: Knopf, 1930), vol. 1, p. 148.

3. Kraus, *Beim Wort genommen* (Munich: Kösel, 1955), p. 164.

Chapter One

1. In an essay on Imre Békessy, *Die Fackel* Nos. 697–705, p. 167.

2. A reference to her is contained in the long poem "Jugend" ("Youth") in *Worte in Versen* (III), p. 180:

> This year we go to the country early,
> on my pale cheek
> I feel your hand.
> You have been gone for a long time.

(Here and in all succeeding quotations from Kraus's poetry, the reference is to *Worte in Versen* [Munich: Kösel, 1959], which incorporates the original nine volumes. The original volume number is given in parentheses.)

3. These include the following from *Worte in Versen:* "Alle Vögel sind schon da" (II), p. 70; "Memoiren" (II), p. 71: "Jugend" (III), p. 178; "Wiedersehn mit Schmetterlingen" (III), p. 118; "Frauenlob" (IX), p. 496.

4. To this sister, Marie Turnovsky, who died in 1933, Kraus dedicated vol. VII of *Worte in Versen.*

5. *Worte in Versen* (II), p. 68.

6. Ludwig Eisenberg, *Das geistige Wien* (Vienna: C. Daberkow, 1893), p. 286.

7. *Fackel* No. 5, p. 11.

8. *Fackel* No. 1, p. 1.

9. *Pro domo et mundo,* in *Beim Wort genommen,* p. 293.

10. "When someone is about to accost me, I hope to the very last moment that the fear of being compromised will keep him from doing

so. But people are determined." *Sprüche und Widersprüche,* in *Beim Wort genommen,* p. 61. "Many people wish to kill me. Many others wish to spend an hour chatting with me. The law protects me from the former." *Ibid.,* p. 63.

11. In a prose piece entitled "Lob der verkehrten Lebensweise" ("In Praise of a Topsy-Turvy Way of Life," 1908), Kraus explains that the objectivity of the sun, which shines on the just and the unjust alike, has become unbearable to him. "Stupidity is asleep, and that's when I go to work. In the distance there is a sound like the noise of presses: stupidity is snoring. . . . When the first morning paper appears on the eastern horizon of culture, I go to bed. . . . And when I awaken, I spread the whole paper shame of mankind before me so that I may know what I have missed, and then I am happy."—*Die chinesische Mauer* (Munich: Langen-Müller, 1964), pp. 168ff.

12. Kraus favored the Cafés Pucher, Parsifal, Imperial, Lebmann, Attaché, Löwenbräu, Fichtehof, and Schellinghof.

13. "Karl Kraus," in Benjamin's *Schriften* (Frankfurt: Suhrkamp, 1955), II, 175.

14. "Die Welt ist durch das Sieb des Worts gesiebt"—"Der Irrgarten," *Worte in Versen* (II), p. 83.

15. An old typesetter had trained a younger man, and these two worked almost exclusively (and proudly) on Kraus's manuscripts in the printshop of Jahoda & Siegel. Both men died within six months after Karl Kraus's demise.

16. *Nachts,* in *Beim Wort genommen,* p. 327.

17. Frank Field, *The Last Days of Mankind: Karl Kraus and His Vienna* (New York: St. Martin's Press, 1967), p. 242.

18. Karl Kraus, *Poems,* translated by Albert Bloch (Boston: Four Seas, 1930), p. 129. (Here as elsewhere, Bloch's revisions of the published text have been used.) The original, "Nächtliche Stunde," is in *Worte in Versen* (VII), p. 381. A musical setting of this poem by Eugen Auerbach appeared in 1929.

19. *Beim Wort genommen,* p. 33.

20. "In a most skillfully worded, unpublished letter of February 1914, Rainer Maria Rilke tries to warn the woman who was considering marriage to Karl Kraus against a 'very continuous association' with the 'excellent writer to whom you are close.' The word 'Jew' does not appear even once in this letter of many pages and many meanings. But it stalks about everywhere between the lines, instils mistrust in the trusting woman, ensnares the distant 'Sidie' with well-sounding admonitions, finely-polished arguments and alarms, and gives rise to scruples. That Karl Kraus *can* (the word is underlined twice in the letter) at bottom be nothing but a stranger to her; his way of life and hers are completely different . . . Rilke achieves what he set out to do with this letter: 'Sidie' Nadherny allows him to change her mind. Under his

influence she abandons the idea of marriage to her beloved friend."—
Ilse Blumenthal-Weiss, "Rilke and the Jews," *Jewish Frontier,* XXVI
(1959), 18.

21. *Worte in Versen* I is dedicated to "Sidonie Freiin Nadherny von
Borutin"; II, "To the Garden of Janovice Castle"; IV, "To the Day of
Vallorbe."

22. Cf. W. Kraft, *Karl Kraus* (Salzburg: Otto Müller, 1956), pp.
337ff. Sidonie Nadherny precipitously fled from Czechoslovakia upon
the Communist takeover in 1948 and went to England, where she died
in 1950, aged sixty-five.

23. Leopold Liegler, *Karl Kraus und sein Werk* (Vienna: R. Lanyi,
1920), p. 239.

24. Paul Schick, *Karl Kraus* (Hamburg: Rowohlt, 1965), pp. 92—93.

25. Kraus, *Die letzten Tage der Menschheit* (Munich: Kösel, 1957),
p. 10.

26. *Weltgericht* is dedicated to their memory. In his obituary of
Franz Janowitz, Kraus wrote: "The narrow field of my human
intercourse, so frightfully inserted into in the wide field of inhumanity,
is rather desolate now that even this light has been extinguished for
me."—*Weltgericht* (Munich: Langen-Müller, 1965), p. 161.

27. *Fackel* Nos. 501—7, p. 17.

28. *Mit vorzüglicher Hochachtung* (Munich: Kösel, 1962), p. 84.

29. Cf. "Vom grossen Welttheaterschwindel" ("About the Great
World Theater Swindle"), in *Unsterblicher Witz* (Munich: Kösel, 1961),
p. 219, and the poem "Bunte Begebenheiten" ("Colorful Goings-On"),
Worte in Versen (VII), p. 409. "I once left the Jewish religious
community in which I found myself through the unfortunate accident
of birth to let a devil's seduction, following a period of comfortable and
never sufficiently appreciated non-affiliation, bring me into the fold of
the church which claims the monopoly of all means of grace."
(*Unsterblicher Witz,* p. 220.) Elsewhere Kraus wrote: "I am not Jew
enough to be a Christian." ("Nach zwanzig Jahren," *Worte in Versen*
[V], p. 257).

30. *Fackel* Nos. 657—67. pp. 1—4.

31. *Worte in Versen* (IX), p. 516.

32. *Fackel* Nos. 876—84 (1932), p. 1.

33. Quoted by Schick, *op. cit.,* pp. 129—30.

34. *Fackel* Nos. 890—905 (1934), p. 141.

35. *Ibid.,* p. 168.

36. Quoted by Schick, *op. cit.,* p. 136.

37. Helene Kann, "Erinnerungen an Karl Kraus," *National-Zeitung*
(Basel), April 22, 1944.

38. Quoted by Heinrich Fischer in "Some Personal Memories of
Kraus, Lasker-Schüler and Brecht," a talk delivered at Balliol College
(unpublished manuscript).

39. Erich Heller, "Karl Kraus. Satiriker, Dichter, Erzieher seiner Zeit." *Hamburger Akademische Rundschau*, December, 1947.

40. *Beim Wort genommen*, p. 270.

41. *Ibid.*, p. 167.

42. *Worte in Versen* (VIII), p. 455.

Chapter Two

1. Robert Scheu, *Karl Kraus* (Vienna: Jahoda & Siegel, 1909), p. 4.

2. *Widerschein der Fackel* (Munich: Kösel, 1956), pp. 332–33.

3. The new edition of the complete *Fackel*, which the Kösel-Verlag began to issue in the fall of 1968, is to consist of thirty-nine volumes with a total of twenty-three thousand pages.

4. *Fackel* No. 1, p. 3.

5. Before, during, and after Kraus's lifetime there were several other periodicals called *Die Fackel*, including a nineteenth-century publication of Hans von Bülow, a Frankfurt scandal sheet, the weekly of the Berlin Socialists, and a publication in present-day Vienna.

6. *Beim Wort genommen*, p. 284.

7. *Widerschein der Fackel* (Munich: Kösel, 1956), p. 39.

8. *Fackel* Nos. 557–60, p. 45.

9. *Die chinesische Mauer*, p. 192.

10. *Ibid.*, p. 195.

11. *Ibid.*

12. *Die Sprache* (Munich: Kösel, 1954), p. 370.

13. At first the headings were *Abfälle (Scraps), Tagebuch (Diary), Persönliches (Personalia), Kehraus (Last Dance, or Cleanup), Vorurteile (Prejudices),* and *Illusionen.* Later *Sprüche und Widersprüche (Dicta and Contradictions)* was used, and this became the title of Kraus's first collection of aphorisms.

14. *Mit vorzüglicher Hochachtung* (Munich: Kösel, 1962), p. 252.

15. *Untergang der Welt durch schwarze Magie* (Munich: Kösel, 1960), p. 114.

16. H. Wickham Steed, *The Hapsburg Monarchy* (London, 1914), p. 192.

17. J. P. Stern, "Karl Kraus's Vision of Language," *Modern Language Review*, LXI (1966), 73.

Chapter Three

1. *Beim Wort genommen*, p. 280.

2. Carl E. Schorske, "Politics and Psyche in *fin de siècle* Vienna: Schnitzler and Hofmannsthal," *American Historical Review*, LXVI (1961), 931.

3. "Den Brüdern," dedicated to Leopold Andrian, from George's *Der Teppich des Lebens* (1900).

4. R. Musil, *The Man Without Qualities* (New York: Coward McCann, 1953), pp. 32–34.

5. "Franz Ferdinand und die Talente" (1914), *Untergang der Welt durch schwarze Magie*, p. 418.

6. *Worte in Versen* (V), p. 258.

7. *Die demolirte Literatur* (Vienna: A. Bauer, 4th ed., 1899), p. 3.

8. *Ibid.*, p. 15.

9. *Ibid.*, p. 17.

10. In 1901 Kraus lost a suit which had been brought against him by Hermann Bahr, whom he had accused of venality, and Emmerich Bukovics, the director of the Deutsches Volkstheater, whom he had charged with breaking his promise to a young author named Rudolf Holzer. A fatuously "patriotic" open letter written by Bahr to Hugo von Hofmannsthal in August, 1914, inspired Kraus's 1916 essay "Gruss an Bahr und Hofmannsthal" (*Weltgericht*, Munich: Langen-Müller, 1965, pp. 47ff) and Act I, Scene 19, of *Die letzten Tage der Menschheit* (pp. 146ff.). See also "Ich warne das neue Osterreich," *Weltgericht*, pp. 94ff., and "Kriegssegen," *Unsterblicher Witz*, p. 317.

11. *Die demolirte Literatur*, p. 6.

12. *Ibid.*, p. 13.

13. *Beim Wort genommen*, p. 253.

14. *Literatur und Lüge* (Munich: Kösel, 1958), p. 69.

15. *Die demolirte Literatur*, p. 36.

16. *Eine Krone für Zion* (Vienna: Moriz Frisch, 3rd ed., 1899), p. 3.

17. *Ibid.*, p. 4.

18. *Ibid.*, p. 6.

19. *Ibid.*, p. 15.

20. *Ibid.*, p. 20.

21. *Ibid.*, p. 23.

22. *Ibid.*, pp. 23–24.

23. *Ibid.*, p. 20.

24. *Ibid.*, p. 26.

25. *Ibid.*, p. 27.

26. *Ibid.*, p. 30.

27. *Ibid.*, p. 29.

28. *Ibid.*, p. 31.

29. *The Complete Diaries of Theodor Herzl* (New York: Herzl Press–Thomas Yoseloff, 1961), I, 1.

30. *Fackel* Nos. 549–56, p. 138.

31. *Fackel* Nos. 657–67. p. 167.

32. *Beim Wort genommen*, p. 215.

33. Theodor Lessing, *Der jüdische Selbsthass* (Berlin: Jüdischer-Verlag, 1930), p. 43.

34. Hans Weigel, *Karl Kraus* (Vienna: Molden, 1968), p. 16.

35. Berthold Viertel, "Karl Kraus. Ein Charakter und die Zeit," in *Dichtungen und Dokumente* (Munich: Kösel, 1956), p. 259.

36. *Untergang der Welt durch schwarze Magie,* p. 420.

37. "Verbrecherische Irreführung der *Neuen Freien Presse,*" *Untergang,* p. 283.

38. Leopold Liegler, *op. cit.,* pp. 390–91, 399.

39. *Ibid.,* pp. 86–87.

40. *Ibid.,* p. 43.

41. Field, *op. cit.,* p. X.

42. *Ibid.,* p. 66.

43. *Ibid.,* p. 8.

44. *Sittlichkeit und Kriminalität* (Munich: Langen-Müller, 1963), pp. 116–17.

45. *Worte in Versen* (II), p. 109.

46. The reference is to Joshua 10, 12: "Sun, stand thou still upon Gibeon; and thou, Moon, in the valley of Aijalon. And the sun stood still, and the moon stayed, until the nations had avenged themselves of their enemies." Fearing an attack by Joshua, the men of Gibeon obtained through a ruse a covenant of peace with the Israelites. When the deception was discovered, the Gibeonites were cursed and assigned a place of perpetual servitude.

47. Field, *op. cit.,* p. 68.

48. "Er ist doch e Jud," *Untergang,* p. 333.

49. *Rundfrage über Karl Kraus* (Innsbruck: Brenner-Verlag, 1913), p. 28.

50. *Untergang der Welt durch schwarze Magie,* p. 335.

51. *Ibid.,* p. 336.

52. *Weltgericht* p. 150.

53. *Beim Wort genommen,* p. 298.

54. *Fackel* No. 33 (1900), p. 20.

55. *Fackel* Nos. 378–79 (1913), p. 58.

56. *Beim Wort genommen,* p. 361.

57. *Ibid.*

58. *Sittlichkeit und Kriminalität,* p. 71.

59. *Beim Wort genommen,* p. 187.

60. *Ibid.,* p. 51.

61. Kraus played the role of Prince Kungu Poti; Mathilde (Tilly) Newes, later Wedekind's wife, portrayed Lulu; and Egon Friedell made his stage debut in the one-line role of the Police Commissioner. In his introductory address delivered on May 29, 1905, Kraus hailed Wedekind as "the first German dramatist who regained for thought the access to the stage of which it had so long been deprived" and discussed his "powerful double tragedy . . . of the hunted, eternally misunderstood female charm which a paltry world permits only to climb into the Procrustean bed of its idea of morality. . . . In the presentation of a woman whom men think they 'have' while they are being had by

her ... I see a perfect vindication of amorality." (*Literatur und Lüge,* pp. 14, 11, 19–20).

62. Frank Wedekind, *Five Tragedies of Sex* (London: Vision Press, n.d.), p. 214.

63. *Sittlichkeit und Kriminalität,* p. 19.

64. *Ibid.,* p. 11.

65. *Ibid.,* p. 27.

66. *Ibid.,* p. 25.

67. *Ibid.,* p. 27.

68. *Ibid.,* p. 35.

69. *Ibid.,* p. 33.

70. *Ibid.,* p. 150.

71. *Ibid.,* p. 45.

72. *Ibid.,* p. 75.

73. *Ibid.,* p. 105.

74. *Ibid.,* p. 146.

75. *Ibid.,* p. 278.

76. *Ibid.,* p. 165.

77. *Ibid.,* p. 129.

78. *Ibid.,* p. 208.

79. *Ibid.,* p. 226.

80. *Ibid.,* p. 231.

81. *Ibid.,* p. 245.

82. *Ibid.,* p. 134.

83. *Ibid.,* p. 262.

84. *Ibid.,* p. 308.

85. T. W. Adorno, *Noten zur Literatur* III (Frankfurt: Suhrkamp, 1965), 62.

86. *Sittlichkeit und Kriminalität,* p. 303.

87. *Die chinesische Mauer,* p. 32.

88. *Ibid.,* p. 21.

89. *Ibid.,* p. 22.

90. *Ibid.,* p. 35.

91. *Ibid.,* p. 52.

92. *Ibid.,* p. 103.

93. *Ibid.,* p. 104.

94. *Ibid.,* p. 105.

95. *Ibid.,* p. 112.

96. *Ibid.,* p. 248.

97. *Ibid.,* p. 128.

98. Kraus, "Grubenhund und Hakenkreuz," *Unsterblicher Witz,* p. 305.

99. Cf. A. Schütz, *Der Grubenhund* (Vienna: Jahoda & Siegel, 1931).

100. *Die chinesische Mauer,* p. 157.

101. *Ibid.,* p. 162.

102. *Ibid.,* p. 175.

103. *Ibid.,* p. 185.

104. *Ibid.,* p. 187.

105. *Ibid.,* p. 236.

106. *Ibid.,* p. 237.

107. *Ibid.,* p. 262.

108. *Ibid.,* p. 272.

109. *Ibid.*

110. *Ibid.,* p. 211.

111. *Ibid.,* p. 275.

112. *Fackel* No. 86 (1901), p. 10.

113. S. Zweig, *The World of Yesterday* (New York: Viking Press, 1943), pp. 99–100.

114. Kraus read Kierkegaard's *Kritik der Gegenwart (The Present Age)* and other works in Theodor Haecker's translation.

115. H. Hesse, *Das Glasperlenspiel,* in *Gesammelte Dichtungen* (Frankfurt: Suhrkamp, 1957), III, 87.

116. *Fackel* No. 199, p. 1.

117. *Untergang der Welt durch schwarze Magie,* p. 189.

118. *Ibid.,* p. 193.

119. *Ibid.,* p. 195.

120. *Ibid.,* p. 190.

121. *Ibid.*

122. *Ibid.,* p. 191.

123. *Ibid.* Arthur Koestler has said about the feuilleton that "it was a perverse blend of travelogue, essay, and short story, bringing out the worst side of each" (*Arrow in the Blue,* London 1952, p. 171). Kraus did except Ludwig Speidel, Ferdinand Kürnberger, and Alfred Polgar from his strictures, since they were, in his opinion, more artistic practitioners of the form.

124. Kraus agreed with his friend, the architect Adolf Loos ("one of the rare anti-Viennese," *Untergang,* p. 425) that cultural evolution was tantamount to the removal of ornaments from articles of daily use.

125. *Untergang der Welt durch schwarze Magie,* p. 197.

126. *Ibid.,* p. 202.

127. *Ibid.,* p. 204.

128. *Ibid.,* p. 205.

129. *Ibid.,* p. 209.

130. *Ibid.,* p. 210.

131. *Ibid.,* p. 205.

132. *Ibid.,* p. 212.

133. *Ibid.,* p. 213.

134. *Ibid.,* p. 425.

135. *Ibid.*, p. 11.
136. *Ibid.*, p. 16.
137. Translated by Albert Bloch, *op. cit.*, p. 49 ("Die Zeitung," *Worte in Versen* [VI], p. 360).
138. *Untergang der Welt durch schwarze Magie*, p. 100.
139. *Ibid.*, p. 93.
140. *Ibid.*, pp. 93–94.
141. *Fackel* No. 287. p. 11.
142. Hans Weigel, *Karl Kraus*, p. 11.

Chapter Four

1. "Language," translated by Albert Bloch, *op. cit.*, p. 118; "Die Sprache," *Epigramme* (Vienna-Leipzig: Verlag "Die Fackel," 1927), p. 96.
2. *Beim Wort genommen*, p. 293.
3. Afterword to *Die Sprache* (Munich: Kösel, 1954), p. 441.
4. J. P. Stern, "Karl Kraus's Vision of Language," *op. cit.*, p. 75.
5. *Beim Wort genommen*, p. 431.
6. *Ibid.*, p. 294.
7. *Worte in Versen*, p. 79.
8. *Beim Wort genommen*, p. 434.
9. Quoted in J. P. Stern, *Lichtenberg: A Doctrine of Scattered Occasions* (Bloomington: Indiana University Press, 1959), p. 164.
10. *Die Sprache*, p. 437.
11. L. Liegler, *op. cit.*, p. 313.
12. L. Liegler, *Karl Kraus und die Sprache* (Vienna: R. Lanyi, 1918), pp. 6–7.
13. J. P. Stern, *op. cit.*, p. 80.
14. *Weltgericht*, p. 10. Kraus's rather inconclusive and unconvincing postwar discussion of the matter (in which he refers to the dual meaning of *"Anschlag"*–"proclamation" or "placard" and "assault") may be found in the *Fackel* Nos. 501–7 (1919), p. 7; Nos. 531–43 (1920), pp. 127ff.
15. J. P. Stern, *op. cit.*, p. 83.
16. *Die Sprache*, p. 438.
17. *Beim Wort genommen*, p. 235.
18. *Ibid.*, p. 238.
19. *Ibid.*, p. 236.
20. *Ibid.*
21. *Ibid.*
22. *Die Sprache*, p. 341.
23. *Ibid.*, p. 96.
24. *Ibid.*, p. 274.
25. *Beim Wort genommen*, p. 413.

26. P. Engelmann, *Letters from Ludwig Wittgenstein* (Oxford: Blackwell, 1967), p. 125.

27. P. Wittgenstein, *Notebooks 1914–6,* ed. by G. H. von Wright and G. E. M. Anscombe (Oxford: Blackwell, 1961), p. 49c.

28. J. P. Stern, *Lichtenberg: A Doctrine of Scattered Occasions,* pp. 163–64.

29. *Weltgericht,* p. 9.

30. J. P. Stern, "Karl Kraus's Vision of Language," pp. 76–77.

31. *Worte in Versen* (II), p. 63.

32. *Beim Wort genommen,* pp. 114–15.

33. What Goethe said of Lichtenberg applies to Kraus as well: his writings are "the most amazing divining rod; wherever he makes a joke, a problem is hidden." (Quoted in *The Lichtenberg Reader,* ed. by F. H. Mautner and H. Hatfield, Boston: Beacon Press, 1959, p. 3.)

34. *Fackel* No. 437, p. 53.

35. *Beim Wort genommen,* p. 324.

36. *Ibid.,* p. 325.

37. *Ibid.,* p. 155.

38. After 1919 aphorisms gave way to epigrams, often extended versions of the same material; these generally appeared in the *Fackel* as *"Inschriften"* (Inscriptions, from 1916 on) and were published in book form in 1927.

39. *Beim Wort genommen,* p. 116.

40. *Ibid.,* p. 238.

41. *Ibid.,* p. 117.

42. *Ibid.,* p. 161.

43. *Literatur und Lüge,* pp. 205–6.

44. *Fackel* No. 349–50, p. 10.

45. *Beim Wort genommen,* p. 332.

46. Translated by Albert Bloch, *op. cit.,* p. 119 (*Worte in Versen* [II], p. 80).

47. *Worte in Versen* (I), p. 12.

48. *Beim Wort genommen,* p. 291.

49. *Ibid.,* p. 338.

Chapter Five

1. W. Benjamin, *op. cit.,* p. 163.

2. *Weltgericht,* p. 26.

3. *Ibid.,* p. 9.

4. "Only the despairer discovered strength in quotations–not the strength to preserve but to cleanse, to tear out of context, to destroy." W. Benjamin, *op. cit.,* p. 192.

5. *Die letzten Tage der Menschheit,* p. 255.

6. In Vienna in 1923 and 1924, in Berlin in 1930.

7. Performances took place at Zurich in 1945 and during the Vienna festival weeks of 1964. A version made for German television has been shown as a film. The Viennese cabaret wit and actor Helmut Qualtinger has preserved his readings from the play on three LP records (Preiserrecords, Vienna).

8. *Die letzten Tage*, pp. 9–10.

9. Leopold Liegler, *Karl Kraus*, p. 262.

10. *Die letzten Tage*, p. 9.

11. M. Spalter, *Brecht's Tradition* (Baltimore: Johns Hopkins Press, 1967), pp. 155, 149.

12. F. Mautner, "Kraus's *Die letzten Tage der Menschheit*." In *Das deutsche Drama*, II (Düsseldorf: Bagel, 1958), p. 376.

13. *Die letzten Tage*, p. 66.

14. *Ibid.*, pp. 71f.

15. *Ibid.*, pp. 75f.

16. *Ibid.*, pp. 79–81.

17. *Ibid.*, p. 86.

18. *Ibid.*, p. 224.

19. *Ibid.*, p. 178.

20. *Ibid.*, p. 197.

21. *Ibid.*, p. 200. The pun appeared earlier in *Sprüche und Widersprüche* (*Beim Wort genommen*, 159).

22. *Ibid.*

23. *Ibid.*, p. 225.

24. See *Die letzten Tage*, Act I. scenes 21, 26; II, 7, 19, 30, 31; III, 2, 33; IV, 10; also *Weltgericht*, p. 164; *Widerschein der Fackel*, p. 155; *Fackel*, Nos. 413–17, p. 36; Nos. 462–71, p. 134.

25. *Die letzten Tage*, p. 750.

26. *Ibid.*, p. 258.

27. *Ibid.*, p. 266.

28. *Ibid.*, p. 331. Cf. "Goethes Volk," *Unsterblicher Witz*, pp. 330ff.

29. *Ibid.*, p. 494.

30. *Ibid.*, p. 237.

31. Kraus's prewar writings contain a number of appreciative remarks about the Emperor.

32. *Die letzten Tage*, p. 303.

33. M. Snell, "Karl Kraus's *Die letzten Tage der Menschheit:* An Analysis." *Forum for Modern Language Studies*, IV (1968), 237.

34. *Die letzten Tage*, pp. 328–29.

35. *Ibid.*, p. 372.

36. *Ibid.*, p. 353.

37. *Ibid.*, p. 459.

38. *Ibid.*, pp. 496–97.

39. *Ibid.*, pp. 497–98.

40. *Ibid.,* pp. 498, 500.
41. *Ibid.,* p. 503.
42. *Ibid.,* pp. 519ff.
43. *Ibid.,* p. 553.
44. *Ibid.*
45. *Ibid.,* p. 562.
46. *Ibid.,* p. 614. Translated by Karl F. Ross.
47. *Ibid.,* p. 615.
48. *Ibid.,* pp. 671; 681.
49. *Ibid.,* p. 670.
50. *Ibid.,* p. 659.
51. *Ibid.,* p. 710.
52. *Ibid.,* p. 766.
53. *Ibid.,* p. 770.
54. M. Spalter, *op. cit.,* p. 148.
55. *Beim Wort genommen,* p. 224.
56. *Weltgericht,* p. 266.
57. *Ibid.,* p. 21.
58. *Ibid.,* p. 272.
59. *Ibid.,* pp. 273, 152.
60. *Ibid.,* pp. 275–76.
61. *Ibid.,* p. 346.
62. M. Snell, *op. cit.,* p. 247.

Chapter Six

1. "I, my homeland's loyal hater,
   Wish from here to go away—
   Blue was ne'er the Danube water,
   But more filthy is the Spree."
Last stanza of "Berliner Theater," 1926; *Worte in Versen* (IX), p. 488.

2. *Worte in Versen* (V), p. 259. Kraus uses a quotation from *Hamlet.*

3. *Mit vorzüglicher Hochachtung,* pp. 90–91, 142.

4. *Fackel,* Nos. 577–82.

5. Henrik Ibsen, *Peer Gynt,* Act II, Scene 7.

6. *Worte in Versen* (IX), p. 517.

7. *Fackel,* Nos. 514–18, p. 43.

8. "Auf einen Polemiker," *Epigramme,* p. 77.

9. *Literatur und Lüge,* p. 77.

10. *Beim Wort gemommen,* p. 322.

11. *Worte in Versen* (III), p. 133.

12. Translated by Albert Bloch, *op. cit.,* p. 106 ("In diesem Land," *Worte in Versen* [VII], p. 382).

13. *Beim Wort genommen,* p. 341.

14. E. Lasker-Schüler, *Briefe an Karl Kraus* (Cologne-Berlin: Kiepenheuer & Witsch, n.d.), p. 100.

15. Kraus's *Epigramme* (1927) are dedicated to Else Lasker-Schüler, and in 1934 she contributed the manuscript of her poem "Ein alter Tibetteppich," one of Kraus's favorites, to *Stimmen über Karl Kraus zum 60. Geburtstag.*

16. *Literatur und Lüge*, p. 148.

17. *Die chinesische Mauer*, p. 53.

18. Cf. *Literatur und Lüge*, pp. 79ff., 99ff., 107ff.

19. *Ibid.*, p. 137.

20. *Prager Presse*, November 27, 1927.

21. H. Nunberg and E. Federn, eds., *Minutes of the Vienna Psychoanalytic Society*, 1908–10 (New York: International Universities Press, 1967), p. 383.

22. *Ibid.*

23. *Ibid.*

24. *Ibid.*, pp. 385–86.

25. *Ibid.*, p. 386.

26. *Ibid.*, p. 388.

27. *Ibid.*, p. 387.

28. *Ibid.*, p. 389.

29. *Ibid.*, p. 391.

30. *Ibid.*, p. 392.

31. *Ibid.*

32. *Ibid.*

33. *Ibid.*

34. S. Freud, *Briefe 1873–1939* (Frankfurt: S. Fischer, 1960), p. 248.

35. *Literatur und Lüge*, pp. 186ff.

36. *Ibid.*, p. 200; 204–5.

37. *Ibid.*, p. 208.

38. *Ibid.*, p. 211.

39. *Ibid.*, p. 213.

40. *Ibid.*, p. 214.

41. *Ibid.*

42. *Fackel*, Nos. 787–94 (September, 1928).

43. *Widerschein der Fackel*, p. 404.

44. *Rundfrage über Karl Kraus*, p. 35.

45. W. Haas, *Die literarische Welt* (Munich: List, 1957), p. 22.

46. *Literatur und Lüge*, p. 238.

47. H. Müller-Einigen, *Jugend in Wien* (Berne: Francke, 1945), pp. 167–68.

48. *Fackel*, Nos. 679–85, pp. 107–8.

49. This version appears in print for the first time; a revised text is contained in *Stimmen über Karl Kraus zum 60. Geburtstag*. Bloch's

own collection *Ventures in Verse* (New York: Frederick Ungar, 1947) contains a section entitled "After the German of Karl Kraus."

50. Kraus, *Poems*, pp. 9, 11.

51. *Rundfrage über Karl Kraus*, pp. 37–38.

52. *Worte in Versen* (II), p. 77.

53. *Die Sprache*, pp. 31ff.

54. *Fackel*, Nos. 484–98.

55. *Fackel*, Nos. 561–67.

56. Werfel, *Spiegelmensch* (Munich: Kurt Wolff, 1920), pp. 188–89.

57. Kraus, *Dramen* (Munich: Langen-Müller, 1967), p. 23.

58. *Ibid.*, p. 59.

59. A. Ehrenstein, *Karl Kraus* (Vienna-Leipzig: Genossenschaftsverlag, 1920), p. 3.

60. *Worte in Versen* (V), p. 326.

61. *Dramen*, p. 32.

62. H. H. Hahnl, "Harald Brüller und Brahmanuel Leiser," *Literatur und Kritik*, Nos. 26–27 (1968), pp. 425–28.

63. *Dramen*, p. 51.

64. *Ibid.*, p. 52.

65. *Ibid.*, pp. 55–56.

66. Translated by Albert Bloch, *op. cit.*, pp. 50–52. The first line of the original (*Dramen*, pp. 56ff.), "Im Anfang war die Presse," inspired Max Vandrey's humorous anthology of journalistic lore, *Am Anfang war die Presse* (Munich: Lama-Verlag, 1961).

67. *Dramen*, p. 67.

68. *Ibid.*, p. 71

69. *Ibid.*

70. *Ibid.*, p. 73.

71. M. Brod, *Streitbares Leben* (Munich: Kindler, 1960), p. 98.

72. M. Brod, *Franz Kafkas Glauben und Lehre.* In *Über Franz Kafka* (Frankfurt: Fischer-Bücherei, 1966), p. 275.

73. K. Wolff, *Autoren, Bücher, Abenteuer* (Berlin: Klaus Wagenbach, n.d.), p. 97.

74. Cf. *Fackel*, Nos. 697–705 (October, 1925), p. 176.

75. *Dramen*, p. 115.

76. Kraus's holograph manuscript is now part of the Samek Collection at the Brandeis University Library.

77. *Dramen*, p. 115.

78. *Ibid.*, pp. 125, 128.

79. *Ibid.*, p. 134.

80. *Ibid.*, pp. 134, 138.

81. *Ibid.*, p. 159.

82. *Ibid.*, pp. 172, 180.

83. *Ibid.*, p. 192.

84. *Ibid.*, pp. 197—98.

85. See the autobiography of Békessy's son, Hans Habe, *All My Sins*, London: G. G. Harrap, 1957. (Original: *Ich stelle mich*, Vienna-Munich-Basel: Desch, 1954.)

86. *Dramen*, p. 201.

87. *Ibid.*, p. 214.

88. *Ibid.*, p. 115.

89. *Ibid.*, pp. 218f.

90. The Schober Song was recorded by Kraus in 1930 and is included, along with "The Press" and other selections, on an LP issued by Preiserrecords, Vienna.

91. *Dramen*, p. 221.

92. *Ibid.*, p. 233.

93. *Ibid.*

94. *Ibid.*, pp. 258, 262.

95. *Ibid.*, p. 265.

Chapter Seven

1. *Beim Wort genommen*, p. 284.

2. *Ibid.*, p. 240.

3. *Worte in Versen* (III), p. 126.

4. L. Liegler, *op. cit.*, p. 403.

5. *Fackel* Nos. 917—22, p. 38.

6. E. Heller, *op. cit.*, p. 243.

7. From an article in the newspaper *Köbenhavn*, November 14, 1911.

8. *Rundfrage über Karl Kraus*, p. 17.

9. W. Benjamin, *op. cit.*, p. 162.

10. Program for a reading of *Wolkenkuckucksheim*, Vienna, November 11, 1923.

11. Heinrich Fischer, ed., *Die Vergessenen* (1926); Ernst Ginsberg, ed., *Ihr Saiten, tönet fort* (1946); Werner Kraft, ed., *Wiederfinden* (1954).

12. Cf. "Der Nobelpreis," *Fackel*, Nos. 800—805 (1929).

13. *Fackel*, Nos. 349—50; the pamphlet was published by Jahoda & Siegel.

14. *Untergang der Welt durch schwarze Magie*, p. 223.

15. *Ibid.*, pp. 224, 243.

16. *Ibid.*, pp. 233, 230.

17. Like his Nestroy adaptations, Kraus's versions of Shakespeare's plays were published by Richard Lanyi, Vienna. The *Sonette* bear the imprint of the Verlag "Die Fackel."

18. Kraus called the versions by Friedrich Gundolf, the dis-

tinguished literary historian in the George Circle, "a standard work of most conscientious Shakespeare disfigurement" (*Die Sprache*, p. 164).

19. Cf. "Sakrileg an George oder Sühne an Shakespeare," *Fackel*, Nos. 885–87 (December, 1932).

20. W. Benjamin, *Illuminations* (New York: Harcourt, Brace & World, 1968), pp. 78, 80.

21. "Vor Macbeth," *Fackel*, Nos. 724–25, contains a critique of earlier Shakespeare translations.

22. R. Flatter, *Karl Kraus als Nachdichter Shakespeares* (Vienna: Berger & Fischer, 1934), p. 86.

23. A. Bloch, "Karl Kraus's Shakespeare," *Books Abroad*, XI (1937), 22.

24. *Ibid.*, pp. 23–24.

25. *Beim Wort genommen*, p. 98.

26. *Fackel*, Nos. 827–33, p. 77.

27. *Beim Wort genommen*, p. 99.

28. *Ibid.*, p. 98.

29. Published by R. Lanyi, the Universal-Edition, and the Verlag "Die Fackel."

30. *Breslauer Neueste Nachrichten*, December 4, 1930.

31. *Anbruch*, March 3, 1929.

32. *Zeitstrophen* (Vienna: Verlag "Die Fackel," 1931), p. 84.

33. *Ibid.*, p. 161.

34. *Ibid.*, p. 194.

35. *Ibid.*, p. 204.

36. *Ibid.*, p. 174.

37. *Unsterblicher Witz*, pp. 85ff.

38. Cf. "Vor dem Einschlafen" (*Worte in Versen* [II], p. 73); "Der Ratgeber" (II), p. 75; "Traum vom Fliegen" (IV), p. 241; "Versäumnis" (V), p. 260; "Traum" (V), p. 263; "Hypnagogische Gestalten" (V), p. 316; "Erlebnis" (VI), p. 343; "Versuch der Erinnerung" (IX), p. 495; "Geheimnis" (IX), p. 498.

39. *Fackel*, Nos. 686–90, p. 37.

40. *Dramen*, p. 81.

41. *Ibid.*, p. 82.

42. *Ibid.*, p. 89.

43. *Ibid.*, p. 491.

44. *Ibid.*, p. 99.

45. *Ibid.*, p. 101.

46. *Ibid.*

47. *Ibid.*, p. 102.

48. *Ibid.*, p. 103.

49. *Ibid.*, p. 106.

50. *Ibid.*

51. *Ibid.*, p. 109.

52. *Ibid.,* p. 110. Berthold Viertel directed his "Truppe" in both dream plays in Berlin in March, 1925, and in Vienna the following month. Lothar Müthel played the poet in both plays and Cäcilie Lvovsky portrayed Imago and the Actress. In Berlin the cast also included Leonhard Steckel and Heinz Hilpert; in Vienna, Carl Goetz and Oskar Homolka joined the troupe. *Traumstück* was also staged in Munich in March, 1928.

53. Caroline Kohn, *Karl Kraus* (Stuttgart: Metzler, 1966), p. 145.

54. *Dramen,* p. 281.

55. *Der Weltfreund (The Friend of the World)* is the title of Franz Werfel's first collection of poetry (1911).

56. *Dramen,* p. 321.

57. *Ibid.,* p. 322.

58. *Ibid.,* p. 336.

59. *Ibid.,* p. 337.

60. *Ibid.,* p. 338.

61. *Ibid.,* pp. 348–50.

62. *Ibid.,* p. 363.

63. *Ibid.,* p. 364.

64. *Ibid.,* p. 366.

Chapter Eight

1. B. Viertel, *op. cit.,* p. 212.

2. *Fackel,* No. 194. p. 11.

3. Kraus actually did screen himself off from most aspects of science and technology, music, the plastic arts, and abstract philosophy. His comment on radio is revealing: "A Viennese janitor tuned into the cosmos" (*Worte in Versen* [VIII], p. 459).

4. In the middle 1920s a group of young Socialists under the leadership of the writer Leo Schmidl, the head of the "Vereinigung Karl Kraus" and founder-editor of *Das Wort* (1924–27), tried to induce the party to join Kraus in his fight against Békessy.

5. *Fackel,* Nos. 864–67, p. 2.

6. W. Benjamin, *op. cit.,* p. 193.

7. Translated by Albert Bloch, *op. cit.,* p. 116. ("Mein Widerspruch," *Worte in Versen* [IX], p. 488.)

8. *Die Dritte Walpurgisnacht* (Munich: Kösel, 1952), p. 9.

9. K. Wolff, *op. cit.,* p. 75.

10. *Fackel* No. 888, p. 4.

11. *Stimmen über Karl Kraus zum 60. Geburtstag,* pp. 11–12.

12. B. Brecht, *Gesammelte Werke* (Frankfurt: Suhrkamp, 1967), IV, 505. In her article "Bert Brecht, Karl Kraus et le Kraus Archiv" (*Études Germaniques* XI [1956], 342–48), Caroline Kohn reports that

Brecht later forgave Kraus and planned to commemorate the twentieth anniversary of his death.

13. W. Alff, "Karl Kraus und die Zeitgeschichte," *Die Dritte Walpurgisnacht* (edition of "Die Bücher der Neunzehn," Munich: Kösel, 1967), p. 319.

14. H. Fischer, "Bemerkung des Herausgebers," *ibid.*, p. 313.

15. *Mit vorzüglicher Hochachtung*, pp. 413–15.

16. *Die Dritte Walpurgisnacht*, p. 10.

17. Kraus disliked being bracketed with Tucholsky. Apart from the fact that he recognized no other satirist, he censured Tucholsky for his wartime writings, his unsympathetic attitude toward Karl Liebknecht and Rosa Luxemburg, and his contributions to publications of the house of Ullstein. Tucholsky committed suicide in his Swedish exile in December, 1935.

18. *Fackel*, Nos. 890–905, p. 25.

19. A recent critic, Fritz Raddatz, has called *Die Dritte Walpurgisnacht* "an intellectual declaration of bankruptcy." ("Der blinde Seher," *Merkur* XXII [1968], 531.)

20. *Die Dritte Walpurgisnacht*, p. 9.

21. *Ibid.*, p. 112.

22. "When he (Strauss) or Herr Furtwängler raises his right arm, one is not quite sure that he is about to conduct." *Ibid.*, pp. 143–44.

23. Wilfried Daim, *Der Mann, der Hitler die Ideen gab*. Munich: Isar-Verlag, 1958.

24. *Die Dritte Walpurgisnacht*, p. 86.

25. *Ibid.*, p. 88.

26. *Ibid.*, p. 151.

27. *Ibid.*, p. 254.

28. *Ibid.*, p. 260.

29. *Worte in Versen* (VIII), p. 435.

30. *Die Dritte Walpurgisnacht*, p. 218.

31. *Ibid.*, p. 225.

32. *Ibid.* (1967 edition), p. 314.

33. *Ibid.*, p. 365.

34. *Ibid.*, p. 20.

35. *Fackel*, Nos. 890–905, p. 312.

36. *Worte in Versen* (III), p. 123.

37. "Abenteuer der Arbeit," *ibid.* (II), p. 64.

38. *Die Sprache*, p. 219.

39. E. Křenek, "Erinnerungen an Karl Kraus," in *Zur Sprache gebracht* (Munich: Langen-Müller, 1958), p. 237.

40. *Beim Wort genommen*, p. 284.

41. *Die Sprache*, p. 342.

42. *Ibid.*, p. 222.

43. *Ibid.*, p. 339.

44. J. P. Stern, *op. cit.*, pp. 81—82.
45. *Stimmen über Karl Kraus zum 60. Geburtstag*, p. 40.
46. J. P. Stern, *op. cit.*, p. 84.
47. *Untergang der Welt durch schwarze Magie*, p. 243.
48. F. Field, *op. cit.*, p. 212.
49. Quoted in W. Kraft, *op. cit.*, p. 13.

An Aphoristic Sampler

The following aphorisms are taken from the collections *Sprüche und Widersprüche* (1909), *Pro domo et mundo* (1912), and *Nachts* (1918). The page references in parentheses are to *Beim Wort genommen* (Munich: Kösel, 1955), which incorporates these collections (on pages 13–178, 181–301, and 305–452, respectively).

I *Self-Portrait*

A good stylist should have narcissistic enjoyment as he works. He must be able to objectivize his work to such an extent that he catches himself feeling envious and has to jog his memory to find that he himself is the creator. In short, he must display that highest degree of objectivity which the world calls vanity. (92)

My writings must be read twice if one is to get close to them. But I don't object to their being read three times. However, I prefer their not being read at all to their being read only once. I would not want to be responsible for the congestions of a blockhead who has no time. . . . One must read all writers twice—the good as well as the bad. The one kind will be recognized; the other, unmasked. (116)

There are writers who can express in as little as twenty pages what I occasionally need as many as two for. (116)

In literary work I find enjoyment, and literary enjoyment becomes work for me. To enjoy the work of another mind, I must first take a critical attitude toward it, i.e., transform reading into work. That is why I shall more easily and more gladly write a book than read one. (119)

It is not easy to get a truly and constantly productive spirit to read. He is to a reader as a locomotive is to a tourist. Also, one does not ask a tree how it likes the scenery. (119)

To write a novel may be pure pleasure. To live a novel presents certain difficulties. As for reading a novel, I do my best to get out of it. (119)

Where shall I find the time to do all this non-reading? (119)

Things might be better if German writers expended one-tenth of the care on their manuscripts which I expend in the printing of my writings. A friend who has often assisted me as a midwife was astonished to see how easy my births were and how arduous my childbed. The others are well off. They work at their desks and enjoy themselves in company. I enjoy myself at my desk and work in company. That is why I avoid company. At the most I could ask people which of the two words they like better. And this is something they don't know. (134)

A man gets so little recognition he could turn into a megalomaniac. (165)

I can say with pride that I have spent days and nights not reading anything, and that with unflagging energy I use every free moment gradually to acquire an encyclopedic lack of education. (166)

Nothing is more narrow-minded than chauvinism or race hatred. To me all men are equal: there are jackasses everywhere, and I have the same contempt for all. No petty prejudices! (59)

If I return some people's greetings, I do so only to give them their greeting back. (370)

Nationalism is the love which ties me to the blockheads of my country, to the insultors of my way of life and the desecrators of my language. (171)

My request that my writings be read twice has aroused great indignation. Unjustly so. My request is a modest one. After all, I do not ask that they be read once. (165)

It so often happened to me that someone who shared my opinion kept the larger share for himself that I am now forewarned and offer people only ideas. (196)

I dreamt that I had died for my country. And right away a coffin-lid opener was there, holding out his hand for a tip. (199)

Let my style capture all the sounds of my time. This should make it an annoyance to my contemporaries. But later generations should hold it to their ears like a seashell in which there is the music of an ocean of mud. (208)

I like to hold a monologue with women. But a dialogue with myself is more stimulating. (32)

If I knew for sure that I shall have to share immortality with certain people, I should prefer a separate oblivion. (68)

From a torch something drops occasionally. A little lump of pitch. (286)

What others offer as an objection often is my premise—e.g., that my polemics attack someone's livelihood. . . . Yet I have never attacked a person for his or her own sake, even if that person was named. . . . This was done only because a name heightens the plastic effect of satire. After ten years of artistic work, my victims ought to be sufficiently trained to see that and stop lamenting. (287)

Am I to blame if hallucinations and visions are alive and have names and permanent residences? (287)

In one ear and out the other: this would make the head a transit station. What I hear has to go out the same ear. (291)

At my desk at night, in an advanced state of intellectual enjoyment, the presence of a woman would disturb me more than the intervention of a Germanist in my bedroom. (293)

A man who feels offended by a satire behaves like the random partner for a night who comes around the next day to claim his personality. Another example has long since taken his place, and at the beginning of another oblivion that man appears with his memories and gets jealous. He is capable of compromising the woman. (321)

Through my satire I make little people so big that afterwards they are worthy objects of my satire and no one can reproach me any longer. (324)

Sorrento, August. For two weeks now I haven't heard a German word or understood an Italian one. This way one can manage to live with people; everything goes like clockwork and no irritating misunderstanding can arise. (63)

Often I prick my hand with my pen and know only then that I have experienced what is written. (430)

When I want to go to sleep, I must first get a whole menagerie of voices to shut up. You wouldn't believe what a racket they make in my room. (430)

I have often been asked to be fair and view a matter from all sides. I did so, hoping that something might improve if I viewed all sides of it. But the result was the same. So I went back to viewing things only from one side, which saves me a lot of work and disappointment. For it is comforting to regard something as bad and to be able to use one's prejudice as an excuse. (430)

I ask no one for a light. I don't want to be beholden to anyone—in life, love, or literature. And yet I smoke. (294)

I hear noises which others don't hear and which interfere with the music of the spheres that others don't hear either. (431)

I already remember many things that I am experiencing. (433)

When I have my hair cut, I am worried that the barber might cut one of my thoughts. (64)

Solitude would be an ideal state if one were able to pick the people one avoids. (68)

An acquaintance of mine told me that reading one of my essays aloud gained him a wife. I count this among my greatest successes. How easily I could have been in this unfortunate situation myself. (34)

The world is a prison in which solitary confinement is preferable. (68)

When I take up my pen, nothing can happen to me. Fate, remember that. (294)

Kokoschka has made a portrait of me. It could be that those who know me will not recognize me; but surely those who don't know me will recognize me. (254)

II *Language and Literature*

The most incomprehensible talk comes from people who have no other use for language than to make themselves understood. (66)

Language is the material of the literary artist, but it does not belong to him alone, whereas color belongs exclusively to the painter. Therefore people ought to be prohibited from talking. Sign language would be entirely sufficient for the ideas which they have to communicate to one another. Are we permitted constantly to smear oil colors over our clothes? (113)

. . . The unfortunate thing is that verbal art works with a material that the rabble handles every day. That is why literature is beyond help. The farther it removes itself from comprehensibility, the more importunately do people claim their material. The best thing would be to keep literature secret from the people until there is a law that prohibits people from using language, permitting them only to use sign language in urgent cases. (233)

"He masters the German language"—that is true of a salesman. An artist is a servant of the word. (116)

A linguistic work translated into another language is like someone going across the border without his skin and putting on the local garb on the other side. (245)

One can translate an editorial but not a poem. For one can go across the border naked but not without one's skin, for, unlike clothes, one cannot get a new skin. (245)

I have decided many a stylistic problem first by my head, then by heads or tails. (292)

I master only the language of others. Mine does what it wants with me. (326)

When I don't make any progress, I have bumped against the wall of language. Then I draw back with a bloody head. And would like to go on. (326)

People don't understand German. But I can't tell things to them in journalese. (165)

Most writers have no other quality than the reader: taste. But the latter has the better taste, because he does not write—and the best if he does not read. (336)

A bibliophile has approximately the same relationship to literature as a philatelist has to geography. (345)

In the beginning was the review copy, and a man recieved it from the publisher. Then he wrote a review. Then he wrote a book which the publisher accepted and sent on to someone else as a review copy. The man who received it did likewise. This is how modern literature came into being. (127)

Today's literature: prescriptions written by patients. (331)

III *Men and Women*

Nothing is more unfathomable than the superficiality of women. (14)

A man's eroticism is a woman's sexuality. (15)

A seducer who boasts of initiating women into the mysteries of love is like a stranger who arrives at the railroad station and offers to show the tourist guide the local sights. (15)

They treat women like a refreshing potion, refusing to admit that a woman may be thirsty. (15)

A woman whose sensuality never ceases and a man who constantly has ideas: two human ideals which mankind regards as sick. (20)

She had such a sense of shame that she blushed when she was caught committing no sin. (30)

A woman occasionally is quite a serviceable substitute for masturbation. It takes an abundance of imagination, to be sure. (33)

Moral responsibility is what is lacking in a man when he demands it of a woman. (40)

The triumph of morality: A thief who has broken into a bedroom claims his sense of shame has been outraged, and by threatening the occupants with exposure of an immoral act he blackmails them into not bringing charges for burglary. (43)

Christianity has enriched the erotic meal with the appetizer of curiosity and spoiled it with the dessert of remorse. (53)

"Women's rights" are men's duties. (51)

The immorality of men triumphs over the amorality of women. (46)

Chastity always takes its toll. In some it produces pimples; in others, sex laws. (44)

Greek thinkers did not disdain whores. Germanic merchants cannot live without ladies. (53)

The superman is a premature ideal, one that presupposes man. (57)

What a world this is in which men reproach women with fulfilling their heart's desire! (192)

I am not for women but against men. (272)

I once knew a Don Giovanni of continence whose Leporello wasn't even capable of compiling a list of unapproachable women. (272)

Sex education is legitimate in that girls cannot be taught soon enough how children don't come into the world. (307)

The conjugal bedroom is the co-existence of brutality and martyrdom. (315)

The slave! She does with him just as he pleases. (316)

He forced her to do her bidding. (316)

A woman must look so smart that her dumbness constitutes a pleasant surprise. (318)

It is considered normal to hold virginity sacred in general and to lust for its destruction in particular. (27)

Virginity is the ideal of those who want to deflower. (41)

Society needs women with a bad character. Those who have no character are a dubious element. (40)

There is no more unfortunate creature under the sun than a fetishist who yearns for a woman's shoe and has to settle for the whole woman. (28)

IV *Journalists and Analysts*

It is the mission of the press to disseminate intellect and at the same time destroy the receptivity to it. (76)

There is a shortage of clerks. Everyone is going into journalism. (78)

In a well-run mental household there ought to be a thorough cleaning at the threshold of consciousness a few times a year. (172)

The making of a journalist: no ideas and the ability to express them. (212)

It would be possible to get along with the perfect feuilletonists if they did not have their eye on immortality. They know how to present the values of others and have at their fingertips everything that they don't have in their heads, frequently showing good taste. If you want a window decorated, you don't call in a lyric poet. He might be able to do the work, but he doesn't. It is a window decorator's job, and this is what gives him a social status which the poet justly envies him. A window decorator can come to the attention of posterity too—but only if the poet writes a poem about him. (218)

A certain psychoanalysis is the occupation of lustful rationalists who trace everything but their occupation to sexual causes. (222)

A journalist is stimulated by a deadline. He writes worse when he has time. (239)

Psychoanalysts are father confessors who like to listen to the sins of the fathers as well. (348)

The trading mentality is said to have evolved in the confines of the ghetto streets. In freedom they indulge in psychology.... What miracles a combination of trading mentality and psychology can produce we see every day. (349)

They have the press, they have the stock exchange, now they also have the subconscious! (223)

Psychology is a bus that accompanies an airplane. (349)

Your conscious probably hasn't much use for my unconscious. But I have implicit faith in my unconscious; it will be able to cope with your conscious. (350)

An analyst turns man into dust. (343)

Psychoanalysis: a rabbit that was swallowed by a boa constrictor just wanted to see what it was like in there. (350)

They pick our dreams as if they were our pockets. (352)

The highest position of trust: father confessor for sins not committed. (30)

Psychoanalysis is that mental illness for which it regards itself as therapy. (351)

V *Miscellany*

Diplomacy is a game of chess in which the nations are checkmated. (419)

War is, at first, the hope that one will be better off; then, the expectation that the other fellow will be worse off; then, the satisfaction that he isn't any better off; and, finally, the surprise at everyone's being worse off. (445)

They judge lest they be judged. (45)

A gourmet once told me that he preferred the scum of the earth to the cream of society. (268)

The whistle-stops are very proud of the fact that the express trains have to pass them by. (268)

He died, bitten by the Aesculapian serpent. (158)

You would be surprised how hard it often is to translate an action into thought. (162)

Truth is a clumsy servant that breaks the dishes while cleaning them. (168)

The ugliness of our time has retroactive force. (230)

Religion, morality, and patriotism are feelings that are manifested only when they are outraged. (59)

When there were no human rights, the exceptional individual had them. That was inhuman. Then equality was created by taking the human rights away from the exceptional individual. (72)

Prussia: freedom of movement with a muzzle. Austria: an isolation cell in which screaming is allowed. (137)

The devil is an optimist if he thinks he can make people meaner. (267)

A weak man has doubts before a decision; a strong man has them afterwards. (292)

To be human is erroneous. (300)

The real truths are those that can be invented. (298)

A sorcerer's apprentice seems to have utilized the absence of his master. But now there is blood instead of water. (371)

Democracy means the permission to be everyone's slave. (214)

Medicine: "Your money and your life!" (158)

Satire chooses and knows no objects. It arises by fleeing from them and their forcing themselves upon it. (287)

The unattractive thing about chauvinism is not so much the aversion to other nations, but the love of one's own. (59)

Critics have a right to be modest and a duty to be vain. (96)

What is the Ninth Symphony compared to a pop tune played by a hurdy-gurdy and a memory! (96)

Life is an effort that deserves a better cause. (299)

I have a shattering bit of news for the esthetes: Old Vienna was new once. (257)

"In this war we are dealing . . ." "Yes indeed, in this war we are dealing!" (387)

The opera: consistency of character and reality of events are qualities which need not be accompanied by music. (98)

I do not trust the printing press when I deliver my written words to it. How a dramatist can rely on the mouth of an actor! (101)

The only art in which the public has a sound judgment is dramatic art. An individual spectator, especially a critic, talks nonsense, but all spectators together are right. It is just the other way round with literature. (101)

Once the decorations were of cardboard and the actors were genuine. Now the decorations don't give rise to any doubt and the actors are of cardboard. (103)

It is better not to express what one means than to express what one does not mean. (121)

Experiences are savings which a miser puts aside. Wisdom is an inheritance which a wastrel cannot exhaust. (168)

The development of technology will leave only one problem: the infirmity of human nature. (373)

If the earth had any idea of how afraid the comet is of contact with it! (277)

Lord, forgive them, for they know what they do! (163)

Selected Bibliography

The standard reference work is the *Karl Kraus-Bibliographie* by Otto Kerry, published by the Kösel Verlag, Munich, in 1970. (An earlier version appeared in Vienna in 1954). Extensive bibliographies are contained in the books by Caroline Kohn and Wilma Iggers (see below). Valuable bibliographical information may be found in the special Karl Kraus issue of *Nachrichten aus dem Kösel Verlag*, Spring, 1964.

PRIMARY SOURCES

1. Kraus's Writings in Book Form

Die demolirte Literatur. Vienna: A. Bauer, 1897.
Eine Krone für Zion. Vienna: Moriz Frisch, 1898.
Sittlichkeit und Kriminalität. Vienna: Leopold Rosner, 1908.
Sprüche und Widersprüche. Munich: Albert Langen, 1909.
Heine und die Folgen. Munich: Albert Langen, 1910.
Die chinesische Mauer. Munich: Albert Langen, 1910.
Pro domo et mundo. Munich: Albert Langen, 1912.
Worte in Versen. Leipzig: Verlag der Schriften von Karl Kraus (vol. I, 1916; II, 1917; III, 1918; IV, 1919; V, 1920).
Worte in Versen. Vienna-Leipzig: Verlag "Die Fackel" (vol. VI, 1922; VII, 1923; VIII, 1925; IX, 1930).
Weltgericht, vol. I, II. Leipzig: Verlag der Schriften von Karl Kraus, 1919.
Ausgewählte Gedichte. Leipzig: Verlag der Schriften von Karl Kraus, 1920.
Literatur oder Man wird doch da sehn. Vienna-Leipzig: Verlag "Die Fackel," 1921.
Die letzten Tage der Menschheit. Vienna-Leipzig: Verlag "Die Fackel," 1922.
Untergang der Welt durch schwarze Magie. Vienna-Leipzig: Verlag "Die Fackel," 1922.
Traumstück. Vienna-Leipzig: Verlag "Die Fackel," 1923.

Wolkenkuckucksheim. Vienna-Leipzig: Verlag "Die Fackel," 1923.
Traumtheater. Vienna-Leipzig: Verlag "Die Fackel," 1924.
Epigramme (compiled by Viktor Stadler). Vienna-Leipzig: Verlag "Die Fackel," 1927.
Die Unüberwindlichen. Vienna-Leipzig: Verlag "Die Fackel," 1928.
Literatur und Lüge. Vienna-Leipzig: Verlag "Die Fackel," 1929.
Zeitstrophen. Vienna-Leipzig: Verlag "Die Fackel," 1931.
Die Sprache (edited by Philipp Berger). Vienna-Leipzig: Verlag "Die Fackel," 1937.

2. Postwar Collections (edited by Heinrich Fischer)

(Volumes I to X were issued by the Kösel Verlag, Munich; Volumes XI to XIV bear the imprint of Albert Langen-Georg Müller, Munich).

I. *Die Dritte Walpurgisnacht*, 1952.
II. *Die Sprache*, 1954.
III. *Beim Wort genommen*, 1955.
IV. *Widerschein der Fackel*, 1956.
V. *Die letzten Tage der Menschheit*, 1957.
VI. *Literatur und Lüge*, 1958.
VII. *Worte in Versen*, 1959.
VIII. *Untergang der Welt durch schwarze Magie*, 1960.
IX. *Unsterblicher Witz*, 1961.
X. *Mit vorzüglicher Hochachtung*, 1962.
XI. *Sittlichkeit und Kriminalität*, 1963.
XII. *Die chinesische Mauer*, 1964.
XIII. *Weltgericht*, 1965.
XIV. *Dramen*, 1967.

SECONDARY SOURCES

1. Books, Pamphlets, Dissertations

BIN GORION (i.e., BERDYCZEWSKI), EMANUEL. *Der Fackel-Reiter: Ein Wort über Karl Kraus*. Berlin: Morgenland-Verlag, 1932. A pamphlet full of vilification.
BORRIES, MECHTHILD. *Ein Angriff auf Heinrich Heine. Kritische Betrachtungen zu Karl Kraus*. Stuttgart: Kohlhammer, 1970. A study of Kraus's attitude toward Heine.
EHRENSTEIN, ALBERT. *Karl Kraus*. Vienna-Leipzig: Genossenschaftsverlag, 1920. A polemical pamphlet.
ENGELMANN, PAUL. *Dem Andenken an Karl Kraus*. Tel Aviv: The Author, 1949. Reissued Vienna: Verlag O. Kerry, 1967. Contains, in addition to the title essay, several tributes to Kraus in prose and poetry.

FICKER, LUDWIG VON, ed. *Rundfrage über Karl Kraus.* Special edition of *Der Brenner.* Innsbruck: Brenner-Verlag, 1917. A number of brief characterizations.

———. *Denkzettel und Danksagungen,* ed. by Franz Seyr. Munich: Kösel, 1967. Contains Ficker's foreword and afterword to the above collection as well as several essays by Ficker on Kraus.

FIELD, FRANK. *The Last Days of Mankind: Karl Kraus and His Vienna.* New York: St. Martin's Press, 1967. A British historian supplies valuable historical background and places Kraus in the context of his time and his country but neglects him as a literary figure.

FISCHER, HEINRICH. *Karl Kraus und die Jugend.* Vienna: Richard Lanyi, 1934. A pamphlet by Kraus's close associate and present literary executor.

FLATTER, RICHARD. *Karl Kraus als Nachdichter Shakespeares.* Vienna: Berger und Fischer, 1934. In this polemical pamphlet, a prominent translator of Shakespeare criticizes Kraus's adaptations.

HAHNL, HANS HEINZ. "Karl Kraus und das Theater." Dissertation. Vienna, 1947. Contains a complete list of Kraus's translations and adaptations for his *Theater der Dichtung.*

HEIDEMANN, CHRISTEL. *Satirische und polemische Formen in der Publizistik von Karl Kraus.* Dissertation, Berlin, 1958.

IGGERS, WILMA ABELES. *Karl Kraus. A Viennese Critic of the Twentieth Century.* The Hague: Martinus Nijhoff, 1967. A wide-ranging study of all important aspects of Kraus which devotes more attention to clarifying his thought in various areas than to a discussion of his works.

JAROMIR, ROBERT (pseud. of Robert Ungar). *Letzten Endes: Eine Studie über Karl Kraus.* Vienna: Moderna, 1935.

JENACZEK, FRIEDRICH. *Zeittafeln zur "Fackel": Themen, Ziele, Probleme.* Gräfelfing: Edmund Gans, 1965. A valuable chronological and thematic outline of *Die Fackel* and documentary guide to Krausiana. Contains a eulogistic essay by Emil Schönauer.

KIPPHOFF, PETRA. "Der Aphorismus im Werk von Karl Kraus." Dissertation. Munich, 1961. On Kraus as an aphorist.

KOCMATA, KARL F. *Karl Kraus, der Krieg und die Helden der Feder. Ein Beitrag zur Literatur der Gegenwart.* Vienna: Verlag Neue Bahnen, 1916. A pamphlet on Kraus's exemplary attitude during World War I.

KOHN, CAROLINE. "Karl Kraus: le Polémiste et l'Ecrivain, Defenseur des Droits de l'Individu." Paris: Marcel Didier, 1962. A Sorbonne dissertation.

———. *Karl Kraus.* Stuttgart: Metzler, 1966. A thorough and appreciative if somewhat uncritical, repetitious, and not always entirely accurate study. Dr. Kohn has written widely on Kraus under the name of Lotte Sternbach-Gärtner.

———. *Karl Kraus als Lyriker.* Paris: Didier, 1969. A study of Kraus the poet.

KOHN, HANS. *Karl Kraus, Arthur Schnitzler, Otto Weininger. Aus dem jüdischen Wien der Jahrhundertwende.* Tübingen: J. C. B. Mohr, 1962. Jewish aspects of Kraus.

KRAFT, WERNER. *Karl Kraus. Eine Einführung in sein Werk und eine Auswahl.* Wiesbaden: Steiner Verlag, 1952. A booklet in the series *Verschollene und Vergessene* (on neglected and forgotten writers).

———. *Karl Kraus.* Salzburg: Otto Müller, 1956. An impressionistic, delightfully discursive yet searching study of key aspects of Kraus. The interpretations of Kraus's poetry are especially valuable.

KREBS, HELMUTH. *Der Friedensgedanke in den Werken von Karl Kraus.* Dissertation, Vienna, 1952. Kraus the pacifist.

KUBASTA, ELISABETH. "Karl Kraus als Lyriker." Dissertation. Vienna, 1950. Kraus the poet.

KUH, ANTON. *Der Affe Zarathustras.* Vienna: J. Deibler, 1925. This pamphlet contains the witty, malicious speech given by one of Békessy's journalists at the Konzerthaussaal in Vienna.

LIEGLER, LEOPOLD. *Karl Kraus und die Sprache.* Vienna: Richard Lanyi, 1918. A lecture given on Nov. 24, 1917 on Kraus's relationship to language.

———. *Karl Kraus und sein Werk.* Vienna: Richard Lanyi, 1920. For many years the standard book on Kraus and still valuable as a profound study. Its unrelieved orthodoxy and anti-Jewish statements are occasional irritants.

LUSHER, HAROLD E. "Joseph Roth, Robert Musil, and Karl Kraus: Their Image of the Old Monarchy." Dissertation. Johns Hopkins University, 1956.

MOENIUS, GEORG. *Karl Kraus, der Zeitkämpfer sub specie aeterni.* Vienna: Richard Lanyi, 1937. Text of address at memorial evening, Vienna, November 30, 1936.

MÜLLER, ROBERT. *Karl Kraus oder Dalai Lama, der dunkle Priester. Eine Nervenabtötung.* Vienna: L. Heidrich, 1914. (Special edition of *Torpedo*). Anti-Kraus pamphlet.

NAUMANN, MICHAEL. *Der Abbau einer verkehrten Welt. Satire und politische Wirklichkeit im Werk von Karl Kraus.* Munich, List, 1969. A searching study of key aspects of Kraus's work.

OBERGOTTSBERGER, HUGO. "Der Weltuntergangsgedanke bei Karl Kraus." Dissertation. Vienna, 1958. Kraus as an eschatological thinker.

POTSCHKE, JOACHIM. *Die satirischen Glossen von Karl Kraus,
1914–1918.* Dissertation, Leipzig, 1962. On Kraus's short war-
time writings.
REINPRECHT, HANS HEINZ. "Karl Kraus und die Presse." Disserta-
tion. Vienna, 1948. Kraus and his fight against the press.
RYCHNER, MAX. *Karl Kraus. Zum 25. Jahrestag des Erscheinens der
"Fackel."* Vienna: Richard Lanyi, 1924. Pamphlet in com-
memoration of the twenty-fifth anniversary of the *Fackel.*
SCHAUKAL, RICHARD, *Karl Kraus. Versuch eines geistigen
Bildnisses.* Vienna: Reinhold-Verlag, 1933. Also contained in
Schaukal, *Über Dichter.* Munich: Langen-Müller, 1966.
SCHEU, ROBERT. *Karl Kraus.* Vienna: Jahoda & Siegel, 1909. An
early appreciation of Kraus on the tenth anniversary of the
Fackel.
SCHICK, PAUL. *Karl Kraus in Selbstzeugnissen und Bilddokumenten.*
Hamburg: Rowohlt, 1965. An informative and evocative illus-
trated study.
STEPHAN, JOACHIM. "Satire und Sprache. Zum Werk von Karl
Kraus." Munich: Anton Pustet, 1964. A Freiburg dissertation on
linguistic aspects of Kraus's satire.
*Stimmen über Karl Kraus. Zum 60. Geburtstag von einem Kreis
dankbarer Freunde.* A *Festschrift* on Kraus's sixtieth birthday.
Vienna: Richard Lanyi, 1934.
Studien über Karl Kraus. Innsbruck: Brenner-Verlag, 1913. Contains
essays by Carl Dallago, Ludwig von Ficker, and Karl Borromäus
Heinrich.
VIERTEL, BERTHOLD. *Karl Kraus. Ein Charakter und die Zeit.*
Dresden: Kämmerer, 1921. Also contained in Viertel, *Dichtungen
und Dokumente.* Munich: Kösel-Verlag, 1956. An impassioned
appreciation of Kraus, written during World War I.
WAGENKNECHT, CHRISTIAN JOHANNES. *Das Wortspiel bei Karl
Kraus.* Göttingen: Vandenhoeck und Ruprecht, 1965. A study in
depth of Kraus's verbal wit.
WEIGEL, HANS. *Karl Kraus oder Die Macht der Ohnmacht.* Vienna:
Fritz Molden, 1968. A rambling and opinionated but sympathetic
and stimulating study of Kraus the Austrian.

2. Articles and Chapters in Books

ADORNO, THEODOR W. "Sittlichkeit und Kriminalität." In *Noten
zur Literatur* III (Frankfurt: Suhrkamp, 1965), pp. 57–82.
ARNTZEN, HELMUT. "Exkurs über Karl Kraus." In *Deutsche
Literatur im 20. Jahrhundert,* Vol. I. H. Friedmann and O. Mann,
eds. Heidelberg: Rothe, 1961, pp. 244–55.

BENJAMIN, WALTER. "Karl Kraus." In *Schriften* II (Frankfurt: Suhrkamp, 1955), pp. 159–95.

BLOCH, ALBERT. "Karl Kraus's Shakespeare." *Books Abroad*, XI (1937), pp. 21–24.

BROCK-SULZER, ELIZABETH. "Karl Kraus als Stilkritiker." *Teivium* III (1945), pp. 300–315.

CYSARZ, HERBERT. "Karl Kraus." In *Neue österreichische Biographie ab 1915*, Vol. XVI (Vienna: Amalthea 1965), pp. 153–69.

DAVIAU, DONALD G. "The Heritage of Karl Kraus." *Books Abroad*, XXXVIII (1964), pp. 248–56.

——. "Language and Morality in Karl Kraus's *Die letzten Tage der Menschheit*." *Modern Language Quarterly*, XXII (1961), pp. 46–54.

ENGELMANN, PAUL. "Kraus, Loos, and Wittgenstein." In *Letters from Ludwig Wittgenstein, With a Memoir* (Oxford: Basil Blackwell, 1967), pp. 122–32.

FISCHER, ERNST. "Karl Kraus." In *Von Grillparzer zu Kafka (Vienna: Globus Verlag, 1962), pp. 209–28.*

FISCHER, HEINRICH. "Karl Kraus." In *Handbuch der deutschen Gegenwartsliteratur* (Munich: Nymphenburger Verlagsbuchhandlung, 1965), pp. 363–66.

——. "The Other Austria and Karl Kraus," in H. J. Rehfisch (ed.), *In Tyrannos. Four Centuries of Struggle Against Tyranny in Germany* (London: Lindsay Drummond, 1944), pp. 309–28.

FORST DE BATTAGLIA, OTTO. "Karl Kraus." In *Abgesang auf eine grosse Zeit* (Vienna: Herold, 1967), pp. 32–47.

GOBLOT, GERMAINE. "Karl Kraus et la lutte contre la barbarie moderne." In *Revue de l'Allemagne*, III (1929), pp. 325–48.

HÄNSEL, LUDWIG. "Karl Kraus." In *Begegnungen und Auseinandersetzungen mit Denkern und Dichtern der Neuzeit* (Vienna: Österreichischer Bundesverlag, 1957), pp. 201–25.

HANSER, RICHARD. "Karl Kraus: A Torchbearer for His Time." *American-German Review*, XXXIV (1968), pp. 24–27.

HATVANI, PAUL. "Versuch über Karl Kraus." *Literatur und Kritik*, No. 15 (1967), pp. 269–78.

HELLER, ERICH. "Karl Kraus: The Last Days of Mankind." In *The Disinherited Mind* (Cambridge: Bowes and Bowes, 1952; New York: Farrar, Straus and Cudahy, 1957), pp. 235–56. (Revised German version in *Enterbter Geist* [Frankfurt: Suhrkamp-Verlag, 1954], pp. 331–70.)

HENNECKE, HANS. "Einer gegen alle: Ein kritischer Versuch über Karl Kraus." *Neue Deutsch Hefte*, V (1959), pp. 974–88, 1081–96.

KRAFT, WERNER. "Ludwig Wittgenstein und Karl Kraus." *Die Neue*

Rundschau LXXII (1961), pp. 812–44.

———. "Es war einmal ein Mann . . . Über die *Dritte Walpurgisnacht* von Karl Kraus." Merkur, XXII (1968), pp. 926–35.

KŘENEK, ERNST. "Ansprache bei der Trauerfeier für Karl Kraus." "Erinnerung an Karl Kraus." In *Zur Sprache gebracht* (Munich: Langen-Müller, 1958), pp. 224–40.

LESCHNITZER, FRANZ. "Der Fall Karl Kraus." *Neue deutsche Literatur* XI (1956), pp. 59–82.

MAUTNER, FRANZ H. "Kraus' *Die letzten Tage der Menschheit*." In Benno von Wiese (ed.), *Das deutsche Drama*, Vol. 2 (Düsseldorf: Bagel Verlag, 1958), pp. 357–82.

MENCZER, BELA. "Karl Kraus and the Struggle Against the Modern Gnostics." *Dublin Review*, 450 (1950), pp. 32–52.

MUSCHG, WALTER. "Karl Kraus: *Die letzten Tage der Menschheit*." In *Von Trakl zu Brecht* (Munich: R. Piper & Co., 1961), pp. 174–97.

PFEIFFER, JOHANNES. "Karl Kraus." In *Deutsche Literatur im 20. Jahrhundert* (Heidelberg: Rothe Verlag, 1955), pp. 305–20.

RADDATZ, FRITZ, J. "Der blinde Seher: Überlegungen zu Karl Kraus." *Merkur*, XXII (1968), pp. 517–32.

REICHERT, HERBERT W. "The Feud Between Franz Werfel and Karl Kraus." *Kentucky Foreign Language Quarterly*, IV (1957), pp. 146–49.

REIMANN, PAUL. "Karl Kraus." In *Von Herder bis Kisch* (Berlin: Dietz-Verlag, 1961), pp. 99–115.

ROLLETT, EDWIN. "Karl Kraus." In *Österreichische Literaturgeschichte*, E. Castle (ed.), Vol. 4 (Vienna: Carl Fromme, 1937, pp. 1909–30). Advance printing in pamphlet form, 1934.

SCHICK, PAUL. "Der Satiriker und der Tod: Versuch einer typologischen Deutung." In *Festschrift zum 100jährigen Bestand der Wiener Stadtbibliothek*. (Vienna: Verlag für Jugend und Volk, 1956), pp. 200–231.

SIMONS, THOMAS W. JR. "After Karl Kraus." *Salmagundi* 10–11 (1969–70), pp. 154–73.

SNELL, MARY. "Karl Kraus's *Die letzten Tage der Menschheit:* An Analysis." *Forum for Modern Language Studies*, IV (1968), pp. 234–47.

SPALTER, MAX. "Karl Kraus." In *Brecht's Tradition* (Baltimore: Johns Hopkins Press, 1967), pp. 137–55. (Contains a translation of Act I, scene 29, of *The Last Days of Mankind*.)

STERN, J. P. "Karl Kraus's Vision of Language." *Modern Language Review*, LXI (1966), pp. 71–84.

STERNBACH-GÄRTNER, LOTTE. "Karl Kraus als Lyriker." *Deutsche Rundschau*, LXXXVI (1960), pp. 48–62.

TAUCHER, FRANZ. "Glanz der Satire: Karl Kraus und Österreich." In *Die wirklichen Freuden.* Vienna: Forum Verlag, n.d., pp. 88–97.
WOLFF, KURT. "Karl Kraus." In *Autoren, Bücher, Abenteuer: Betrachtungen und Erinnerungen eines Verlegers* (Berlin: Klaus Wagenbach, n.d.), pp. 75–99.
ZOHN, HARRY. "Karl Kraus: Prophet of Protest and Purity of Language," *Jewish Quarterly,* XV (1967), pp. 34–36.
———. "Krausiana: Karl Kraus in English Translation; Current Criticism of Karl Kraus." *Modern Austrian Literature,* III (1970), pp. 25–35.
———. "Das Wort als Waffe: Die Sprache in der Satire von Karl Kraus." *Zeitschrift für die Geschichte der Juden,* VII (1970), pp. 167–71.

Index